Mosley's Old Suffragette

A Biography of

Norah Dacre Fox

Angela McPherson

&

Susan McPherson

First published 2010

Revised Edition 2011

©2011 Angela McPherson and Susan McPherson

All rights reserved

The copyright in the enclosed work entitled

Mosley's Old Suffragette

is jointly owned by Angela McPherson and Susan McPherson and may not be used for any purpose without our express permission. We confirm that we assert our moral rights in the work.

ISBN 978-1-4466-9967-6

Dedicated to Olive, a mother who loved her children above all things and fought hard to protect them in difficult circumstances.

Acknowledgements

We would like to thank Olive James and Christine Elam for sharing their memories; staff at The Women's Library - London Metropolitan University for their generous assistance; Jeffrey McPherson and Jeremy Glyde for their support; Simon Boyce, a distant relative, for his help with Descou ancestry and Philip Coupland for providing otherwise difficult to obtain local newspaper clippings.

After publishing the first edition, grandchildren of Frank Doherty made contact with us. Thanks must, therefore, go to Maureen Meadley, and her family for supplying details which helped to develop and corroborate our understanding of Norah's relationship with her father John Doherty, and the rest of her family. Susan Doherty in particular was particularly assiduous in tracing family members and without her persistence some gaps in the family history would have remained empty.

Contents

PREFACE 1

IRISH ROOTS 7

ALL THAT CROWD: DACRE FOX AND THE PANKHURSTS 29

    Society Woman 29
    Words 34
    Deeds 46
    Ulster Connections 59
    Stone Walls 74

CALLING ALL WOMEN 85

    Patriot Games 85
    Enemy Alien Peril 93
    Qualification of Women Act 104

THE WRONG SIDE OF THE BED 111

    Royal Ancestry 114
    Mr & Mrs Norah Elam 127

THE GOOD BODY 139

FASCISM NEXT TIME 153

WEST SUSSEX BLACKSHIRTS 153
OLD SUFFRAGETTE 177

THE LEADER 197

OFFERINGS OF THE POOR 198
FIFTH COLUMN 206
PUBLICITY AND INNUENDO 214

IF HITLER KILLED SO MANY JEWS 223

A MAN OF INDEPENDENT MEANS 223
INDEPENDENCE DAY (A PERSONAL MEMOIR) 239

POSTSCRIPT 245

BIBLIOGRAPHY 247

PREFACE

'Evelyn, Evelyn, where is Evelyn?' cried my grandmother, angrily tapping her walking cane on the floor as she searched all through the house for my father. Evelyn Anthony Christopher Elam, known as 'Tony' to everyone else, was my father, the only child of Norah Dacre Fox.

Together with my parents and two younger sisters, I lived with Norah from about the age of five until eight years at her home 'Gothic Cottage' in Twickenham. We witnessed her exercise a controlling influence on my father who frequently felt her displeasure. She regularly threatened that she would – or taunted him that she already had – cut him out of her will; in spite of their dependence on each other, they fell out and argued frequently, and were both prone to vicious outbursts of rage towards each other.

While no personal papers, documents, or other artefacts came to her family, my daughter and I have been able to research Norah's life based on publicly available historical records (mainly newspapers and MI5 documents) along with any information that my mother and sister Christine could remember.

Although my mother was into her eighties when we began this research, Christine had spent a large amount of her life living with, and latterly caring for, my mother and so was able to help access her memory slowly over time. My father, whose temper was unleashed on our family too, disappeared for some years when I was 15 and I never saw him again, apart from one occasion briefly, and thus has not been a source of information for this biography. He refused to talk about his mother or elaborate on her activities in anyway except when forced to in the briefest of terms. We later discovered he had set up home with a new family; he died in 1981. I had little memory or interest in Norah's life until my daughter Susan, then 30, rang me out of the blue and asked if the name 'Norah Elam' rang a bell. Discovering things that I had blocked out and largely tried to forget, Susan revived my interest in Norah.

Angela McPherson

I had little interest in my mum's family and ancestry until I was 30. Before then I had stored a small collection of 'facts' in my mind: my great grandmother was a suffragette and was close to the Pankhursts; as a feminist she had chosen not to marry her partner to save her fortune being transferred to her husband; my mum's family was somehow connected to Bernadotte, Napoleon's General; there was some family silver that had gone missing; my mum's father was a tyrant and a bully. This was the sum of my knowledge and the last of these 'facts' was probably the reason I had no interest in pursuing further what might to others seem like fascinating clues for unravelling a thrilling plot. I did always feel a disconnected sense of pride about having a suffragette in the family and in the end it was this lingering feeling that finally hooked one day and I resolved to try and find out more.

A notion took me one day to open Google and type 'Elam suffragette'. These were the only two facts I had to go on, my mum's maiden name being Elam. In the following days I made repeated phone calls to my mum to try and jog her memory, and find out if the woman that seemed to be thrown up by my scatter-gun search approach could be her ancestor. I found myself gradually tapping my mum's memory and finding that as the internet unearthed more and more skeletons, so my mum's memory seemed to have been unlocked. Eventually we also got in touch with my grandmother and Aunt Christine, with whom we had not had contact for many years, and discovered that a wealth of further information lay there to be tapped. A sense of urgency set in given my grandmother's age as she is now possibly one of the only adults alive, who was an adult at the time she lived with and knew Norah. Over the following three years we gathered enough information for the present biography. While this was a fascinating meander through various historical subjects, the pride in the suffragette took a severe knocking and was replaced by a far more complex set of attitudes towards this woman, Norah Dacre Fox, my great-grandmother.

Susan McPherson

'Mrs Dacre Fox' aka 'Norah Elam' appears in a number of academic texts owing to her prominent role as a suffragette and later as a member of the British Union of Fascists (BUF), a rare political path that Norah shared with Mary Richardson and Mary Allen. Historians of female fascists have been keen to try and account for how an individual who fought for votes for women could become a prominent supporter of a fascist organisation which was profoundly undemocratic and masculine in its nature. Those historians have, in their attempts to understand these seemingly strange political choices, analysed recorded evidence (much of it partial or incomplete) along with propaganda materials written by the individuals concerned, to speculate on their motivations and construct explanations of their beliefs or ideology.

The pitfalls of studying political figures in this way were highlighted by Kean in her paper on Mary Richardson[1] in which she 'considers the ways in which autobiography was rewritten to fit various political circumstances and to suggest political continuity and cohesion'. Mary Richardson and Norah were colleagues and co-workers in the Women's Social and Political Union (WSPU) and both became fascists and members of the BUF, together with Mary Allen. The same issues Kean highlights in relation to Mary Richardson's writings arise in trying to understand Norah's political choices primarily using her own writings as source material. This book tries to place Norah's writings in the context of her whole life and family, and hopefully bring some understanding to that life.

Some authors have begun accepting statements about Norah recorded in published work as 'facts'; 'facts' which are then perpetuated with reference to previous publications rather than source material. As a result some myths about Norah have begun to appear, which it is hoped this book will throw light on. The 'facts' held within the family as described above are largely debunked in this book as are some of the published 'facts'. Some of the myths and partial truths found in published work include claims that Norah was a member of the Women's Freedom League; that Norah worked on government commissions during World War one; that Norah was 'Lady' Dacre Fox; that Norah and Dudley Elam were married; that Dudley Elam was a Professor and Don at Oxford; that the couple were wealthy; that Dudley was a 'Chairman' of the Chichester Conservatives, and that Norah was also active in that organisation; that Norah and Dudley were 'invited' to visit Mosley and Diana in Holloway prison in 1943; that MI5 raided Norah's offices at the London & Provincial Anti-Vivisection Society and interrogated her because of her attendance at secret meetings and suspected dealing in Italian money. While some of these statements are partially true, and others completely untrue, the aim in researching and writing this book has been to examine in detail the original source documents that are available and properly contextualise them.

IRISH ROOTS

Norah's father, John Doherty, was born in Ballyshannon, County Donegal, North West Ireland in 1849.[2] His father, Francis Doherty was a moderately wealthy 'Gentleman' with no notable land holdings.[3][4] Whether or not John was born into a Catholic family (which is unknown), John Doherty's first marriage was Catholic and his first two children were baptised into the Catholic faith suggesting he was probably born and brought up as a Catholic.

In 1891, John Doherty reported on the UK census return that he was born within the townland of Camlin. Camlin was situated on the banks of the River Erne upstream from Ballyshannon town centre and was actually the site of Camlin Castle, seat of the Tredennick's, an Anglo-Irish family who had significant land holdings and interests in the area.[5] John also told his children that he had been born in a castle. However, despite a search of papers held by descendants of the Tredennick family, no reference to a Francis or John Doherty could be found connected to Camlin Castle. John Doherty's birth therefore remains a mystery but it is possible that he, like his daughter Norah, occasionally allowed exaggerations of his wealth and status to go uncorrected.

The town of Ballyshannon itself is believed to be one of the oldest settlements in Ireland, and spreads out on either side of the hilly banks of the River Erne where it meets the sea. Ballyshannon saw its greatest expansion during the eighteenth and nineteenth centuries and was at one point a prosperous trading port providing a gateway to south Donegal, Fermanagh and Cavan; all border counties on what eventually became the divide between Northern Ireland and the Republic of Ireland.

Despite this, life was hard in this part of Ireland in the 1850s. 'The Outer Edge of Ulster',[6] a social memoir of the time written by John Dorian a school teacher, described the far reaching changes brought about in Donegal by changing education practices from 1800 onwards. Dorian believed that the main factor affecting education, and the prospects for the population, was that during the early 1800s the majority poor catholic population were taught in Gaelic. The early hedge schools and the 'New Schools' were later brought under the auspices of the Church Education Society. Once English became the main language taught and used in schools a slow social revolution took place, which had profound effects on society. This meant that of the vast numbers of Irish who emigrated during the famines, they were aided by their ability to speak English.

We do not know what level of education John Doherty achieved but it seems safe to assume that he took full advantage of whatever education he received. In addition, a picture emerges of a man who was ambitious and determined to pursue every personal advantage he could. He never let the grass grow under his feet, and took an active political interest in whatever community he lived in, assisted by good networking skills, and an easy ability to communicate.

By the age of 20 John Doherty had left Ballyshannon and was working in Dublin. His first marriage was to Mary Coombe Henwood in 1868.[3] Mary, who was under 21 at the time, was the daughter of John Henwood, a civil engineer, and both Mary and John Doherty were residing at her father's home at Sandymount, Dublin at the time of the marriage. John Doherty was working as a cashier at the time. The marriage took place in a registry office, which was unusual practice at this time.

John and Mary's first child Mary Ada Doherty was born in 1869, just short of nine months after the wedding day, which may explain the hastily arranged marriage in a registry office[7]. The child was baptised into the Roman Catholic Church of St Mary's, Haddington Road, Dublin, at which time John Doherty described his profession as 'clerk'. The couple were still living with Mary's family and only moved to their own family home when their daughter was three.[8] It was at their own home that their second child, Emily Alice Doherty, was born in 1873.[9] Emily was baptised into the same Catholic Church as her sister. By this time, John was working as a 'book-keeper'.

A year later tragedy overtook the marriage when Mary died at home[10] as a result of complications from pregnancy. The child, a little boy named Francis after his grandfather, died from the same infection as his mother, having survived only fourteen days.[11] [12] Later in life, John Doherty would occasionally mention a child who had died, but he did not allow the matter to be discussed in the family and appeared to have harboured anger and bitterness about the child's death. The lasting impression amongst his descendants was that the loss of his wife and child led to a great deal of suppressed anger.[13]

By the time of Mary's death, John was working as a 'commercial traveller', and on his travels met his second wife Charlotte Isabel Clarke who he married at Kinsale, Cork in 1876 just 15 months after Mary's death. Charlotte was a Protestant and John made a hasty conversion in order to marry her in the Church of Ireland Parish Church of the Holy Trinity, Diocese of Cork.[4]

Charlotte had been born 5 March 1849, in Ranelagh, Dublin,[14] and baptised at St Peter's Church, City of Dublin, Church of Ireland. Ranelagh is a residential area on the south side of Dublin, and was named after Ranelagh House, home of the Cole family, who took their title (Earls of Ranelagh) from the district in County Dublin. The district was originally a village just outside Dublin, but was eventually swallowed up by the expanding city around the end of the eighteenth and early nineteenth century. Like Ballyshannon, Dublin is located at the mouth of a river, the Liffey, with the river providing a dividing line between the north and south of the city. In general the north of the river was seen as a working class area and the south as middle and upper class, with the odd exception.

Charlotte's parents were Walter Clarke and Charlotte Evans, who had married in 1832, in the same parish church where Charlotte had been baptised.[15] Charlotte had at least one brother, Thomas Benjamin Clarke, born in Dublin in 1836 who was some 13 years older than her and years later would bear witness to Norah's marriage in London. The Clarke's lived at 11 Mount Pleasant Cottages, Ranelagh, where they rented a house, office and yard, and ran an upholstery business. Upholstery was part of the 'Saddlers, Upholders, Coach and Coach-Harness Makers, Bridle Cutters and Wheelwrights' Guild which was a relatively respectable trade, ranked ninth out of 25 in the hierarchy of Dublin Guilds at that time.[16] This profession afforded the Clarkes a good to above average income and a comfortable lifestyle with the total Net Annual Value of their land and buildings being worth £11 5s 0d.[17]

When Charlotte married John Doherty on 28 March 1876 she was a 27 year old spinster. The difficulties of spinsterhood in this era are well documented, and as a dependent woman with no means of self-support, there is every reason to suppose that for Charlotte and her family, marriage to John Doherty was based on a large measure of convenience for all parties. Taking on the mothering of John Doherty's two older daughters aged seven and two could not have been an easy decision, particularly as they had been baptised Roman Catholic. Charlotte, Mary Ada and Emily Alice must have had a lot of adjusting to cope with.

After the marriage John and Charlotte, together with Mary and Emily, set up home in what is now known as Dublin's Riviera: Dun Laoghaire Rathdown. Around this time John Doherty appears to have given up work as a commercial traveller, and set up business as a paper merchant in Dublin. Charlotte bore John seven children over the next 12 years; Norah (1878), John (1879), Frank (1880), Redmond (1881), Maurice Dermot (1882), Hugh (1884) and Neal Gerald (1886), all born in the Dun Laoghaire Rathdown area, at Booterstown, Blackrock and Stillorgan.

Norah, the oldest of Charlotte's children (but John's third child) was born 5 May 1878[18] while the family were living at 13 Waltham Terrace, Blackrock, Dublin. By the time Neal, their last child was born, the family were living in a house called Garnavilla in Stillorgan. The children were all baptised in the Church of Ireland at Booterstown[19] and probably attended the Booterstown church school. A Church of Ireland family living in Dublin would have been among a minority, but with John Doherty running a successful business as a paper merchant they would not have been unusual.

Dun Laoghaire Rathdown was made up of 18 villages and was set in beautiful countryside with many fine houses and detached villas occupied by various titled landowners and wealthy businessmen.[20] The area was known to be the home of writers, artists, musicians and nationalists including Roger Casemont, Charles Kirkham and Lord Edward Fitzgerald. The steam mailboat packet service transferred to Dun Laoghaire Rathdown in 1826 when it became Ireland's main ferry port. Stillorgan in the 1870s and 1880s was one of 18 villages in Dun Laoghaire Rathdown. According to the Kilmacud-Stillorgan Local History Society, 'it consisted of about 50 terraced dwellings, a few shops, two public houses and two churches. The village was surrounded by dairy farms and large residences set in their own grounds. The farms and large houses provided employment for farm hands, gardeners and domestics for many of the local inhabitants and there was a small number of trades people in the area'.[21]

Garnavilla itself was, 'a medium-sized' family residence on the Kilmacud Road at the west entrance to the village. It was probably built in the late 1700s or early 1800s and stood in a garden with boundary walls. The name relates to an area in Tipperary which reads 'Garran 'a bhilla' in Gaelic. In English, this means 'the grove on the rim'. Before it was demolished in the 1960s, the estate was about half an acre. Garnavilla being a medium-sized estate suggests that John Doherty was moderately wealthy rather than excessively wealthy in Irish terms.

In 1888 at the height of the Land Wars in Ireland, John moved his entire family to London.[8] Charlotte's brother, Thomas Benjamin Clarke, also moved to London[22] and it is possible that other family members made the journey as well. John left Ireland with sufficient funds to set up home in a reasonably large London house called Greenlands, Fairfax Road, Teddington,[23] where they employed a cook, Margaret Waite, whom they had brought with them from Ireland, and a housemaid, Mary

L Wells, whom they employed when they arrived. John brought with him enough funds not only to buy the family home, but also to set up a printing business at 51 Temple Gardens, which he ran until his death in 1929.

Why did John move his family to London in 1888? To understand the factors affecting John's motivations at this time, some understanding of Irish history is required. In the 1700s, England attempted to rid Ireland of Catholicism through repressive laws depriving Catholics of political and social rights, restrictions on their places of worship, and tight control of Catholic clergy. These became known as the Penal Times.[24] However, according to Kee, 'the religious sections of the penal laws were …. applied much less severely in practice than in theory' and Catholicism remained the religion of the majority of the population across most of Ireland. Nevertheless, the country was ruled by the English Protestant monarchy, and those who were born Protestant, or who converted from Catholicism to Protestantism, were the only Irishmen allowed to own land or property. Much land was also given to Englishmen appointed to run local affairs in Ireland on behalf of the monarch, although over the centuries the English and Irish inter-married and merged into one culture.

In 1800 the Act of Union handed the British government total administrative responsibility for running Irish affairs, and saw the Church of Ireland becoming the Established church in spite of it being the minority religion. This status quo enjoyed some peaceful acceptance, but because the English government did little to intervene when Ireland experienced difficulties, feelings against English rule were stirred up during times of hardship. A severe potato blight and famine hit between 1845 and 1849, and the British government failed dramatically to prevent mass starvation among the populace who relied wholly on the potato as their main food source (given that all other crops had to be sold for export for tenants to afford their rents which had escalated over time). This famine and subsequent famines grew in Irish consciousness to become an Irish genocide committed by the English[24] and Irish Nationalism began to flourish. John Doherty and Charlotte Clarke were both born in the final year of the potato blight and famine that began in 1845 and would have had to come from well off families to have survived.

John Doherty Junior, the second child of John and Charlotte Doherty, was born in 1879, a year which saw more famine and threats of evictions of tenant farmers from the land. It was also the year in which the Land League was formed to protect the interests of tenant farmers and to 'boycott' any farmers who accepted new tenancies where the former tenant had been evicted. The Land League was presided over by Charles Stuart Parnell who had been elected to the Westminster parliament in 1875. Although Parnell tried to avoid incitement to violence, he did not discourage the violent means employed by the League. The activities of the Land League reached their height during the period when John and Charlotte Doherty left with their family to settle in England. The social and political upheavals of this time were depicted in the novels A Drama in Muslin,[25] Mount

Music[26] and in Disturbed Ireland by Bernard H Becker, a journalist for the Daily News.[27] These all depict the level of uncontained violence and fear that many Irishmen faced in their daily lives and the growing tensions between landowners and tenants with evictions, and the retributive killings of landlords and their agents.

Traditionally, Nationalism in Ireland has been seen as a Catholic interest and Unionism a Protestant one. Parnell, however, was an Irish Protestant landowner and a land reform agitator; a nationalist political leader who founded and led the Irish Parliamentary Party and a Home Rule MP in Parliament.[24] Prior to Parnell, Smith O'Brien and James Stephens, also heavily involved in pressing for Irish rights, were similarly Protestants. Subsequent to Parnell, during the Dublin Easter uprising in 1916, a prominent Fenian arrested and court-martialled for being a leading member of the rebellion was Constance Markievicz, daughter of the Protestant landowning family the Gore-Booths of County Sligo.

John Doherty was an ardent Irish Nationalist and a founder member of the Dublin Branch of the Irish Protestant Home Rule Association (IPHRA)[28][29] which, although a Protestant organisation, ultimately became anti-Parnellite reflecting splits within the Protestant Home Rule supporters.[30] The IPHRA was formed in Belfast in April 1886 and was followed by the inaugural meeting of the Dublin branch in May 1886, which was attended by John Doherty along with fellow Protestant nationalists including Alfred Webb. Subsequent public meetings attracted famous nationalists including JB Yeats and Maud Gonne the feminist and actress who had a turbulent relationship with WB Yeats.

The IPRHA was formed against the backdrop of a period of febrile political activity in the United Kingdom. 1885 had seen a general election at Westminster, won by Gladstone's Liberal Party (who supported Irish Home Rule), but without an overall majority and with the Irish Nationalists led by Parnell holding the balance of power. This resulted in a year of political turmoil which ended with another general election taking place in July 1886. In this election, the Liberals lost heavily, and their period of dominance of English politics was ended.

It is in this context then that the IPRHA Minutes record that as a committee member John was tasked with leading a delegation to Kingston, England in late June/early July 1886 in support of the prospective Irish Parliamentary Party candidate for Dublin South, Sir Thomas Esmonde, 11th Baronet, who was campaigning there. The Minutes appear to indicate that John had been chosen for the Kingston delegation because of his existing business and political contacts in the area. This information in the IPHRA minutes suggests that John had clearly been exploring possibilities for a move to London around this time and had been increasing his business activity in Kingston and Twickenham as a result. The success of this work meant that he was less involved with the IPHRA committee meetings than they would have liked him to be, an issue also reflected in the Minutes.

The IPHRA, however, clearly valued John's political skills and asked him to address a public meeting on 'Protestantism in an Independent Ireland'. The subject of this proposed address by John reflected the tension between Parnellite and anti-Parnellite factions and the ongoing debate about whether Protestants would retain status and freedom in a free Ireland and not be persecuted by the Catholic majority, which many Protestants feared. John did not accept this invitation however and indeed tried to resign from the Committee on the grounds of his accumulating business trips to London.

According to Loughlin[30] there was a basic 'disharmony' between the Belfast and Dublin groups of the IPHRA from the beginning, the Belfast executive believing the Dublin section to be 'usurpers'. Loughlin suggests the main conflicts between the two sections lay mostly in the fact that Belfast and Ulster provided many of the 'rank-and-file' while the Dublin executive provided the 'intellectual leadership'. In addition the Protestants in the three southern provinces of Ireland felt extremely vulnerable, being a much smaller section of the population than in Ulster. In addition there was a split between Church of Ireland and non-conformist Protestants in the southern provinces. The Church of Ireland adherents were identified as a distinct grouping made up mostly of Anglo-Irish landed society, who owned large tracts of land on which they lived as resident landlords, while '…. urban based clergymen, merchants and doctors, shopkeepers and academics…' tended to be non-conformist (Presbyterians, Methodists for example).

John Doherty as a member of the Church of Ireland but by profession not particularly wealthy may have been sympathetic to both groups.

Loughlin however highlights the biggest difficulty underlying the Protestant Home Rulers position as being that the Nationalist movement was overwhelmingly Catholic, and this carried implications for the standing of a minority Protestant population living in an independent Ireland. It is easy to see why John Doherty, being born into a Catholic family, later converting to Church of Ireland, would be attracted to the IPHRA, but the wrangling and uncertainty identified by Loughlin would probably have given rise to doubts and compounded a possible sense of vulnerability living and working in Dublin. Taken together with the splits identified in the Protestant community and his position within it, John Doherty probably had considerable pause for thought in deciding exactly where he did fit in, and more importantly, how he would be viewed in an independent Ireland under Home Rule.

It seems, therefore, that John Doherty took a pragmatic decision within two years of becoming involved with the IPHRA that his and his family's interests were probably best served by leaving Ireland. Many frustrated nationalists at that time immigrated to America, but John Doherty chose to move his family and settle in England. Several of John's children later continued the journey to America, but Norah remained in England and in later life crossed paths in various ways with some of the prominent Irish leaders involved in the ongoing struggle for Irish independence. John Doherty's motivations and decision making were often demonstrated to have been based on pragmatic principles, and on this basis he probably chose England simply because he had a large family and England was the most easily accessible and convenient place to settle for business and financial reasons.

Norah was 10 years old when the family arrived in London. We know very little about her education either before or after this except that her later writings and speeches suggest that she received some formal education. This may have included training in oratory and pronunciation, and she also probably received training in typewriting given her work as a typewriting supervisor in 1917. In adult life Norah spoke in Received Pronunciation in spite of her Irish roots. While many suffragette women received training in oratory, it seems unlikely that Norah was trained by the suffragettes, given that she arrived in the Women's Social and Political Union (WSPU) with these skills already in hand, helping her to make a marked impact very quickly.

John Doherty was reported by Norah to have been a strict disciplinarian, especially where his wife and daughters were concerned. John Doherty had kept a large number of guard dogs at Garnavilla before the family move to England, and Norah once got slashed across the face with a whip that John had been using on the dogs.[31] This incident and her father's strict discipline were burned into Norah's character and memory, and she grew to hate her father and desire revenge for his treatment of her, her sisters and mother. Norah adored her mother, and felt that John treated Charlotte very badly in a degrading way like a child and a possession, expected to be subservient at all times. Meal times in the family home were observed strictly in accordance with John Doherty's rules, these being that only men were permitted to talk at the table. The boys were not spared from John's cruelty though, and according to Norah, one of her brothers committed suicide because of her father's treatment of him. There is, however, no record of such a suicide, and as we shall see, all the children of the family have been traced and accounted for.

John Doherty's temperament gained some minor infamy in The Times in 1897[32] in the case of Francis Arthur Wells who was the younger cousin of Mary L Wells, the Doherty's housemaid. Francis and Mary's fathers (Andrew and Arthur Wells) were brothers, both from Teddington, who worked as house painters.[33] Francis began taking regular train journeys on the London and South Western Railway Company (to where and for what reason is unknown). He could not afford the fares and so whenever he was asked to show his ticket he used what he knew of the Doherty family to impersonate John Doherty Junior who happened to hold a season ticket. Along with personal and address details, Francis had obtained a letter written by John Doherty Senior stating that John Doherty was his father. He was eventually caught out and summoned to appear in court on six charges of defrauding by 'travelling on the line without paying his fare with intention to avoid payment, and for giving a false name and address'. When John

Doherty Junior was called to the stand, he swore 'that his father was a hot-tempered Irishman, and there would be the devil to pay for treating him like that'. The defendant was found guilty and fined. It seems that Mary was dismissed from the Doherty's employ after this incident, but in later life Norah employed Florence Wells, another of Mary's cousins, as a housemaid, perhaps as a sign of disapproval of her father's treatment of the Wells family.

While we know little of Norah's education, we can speculate on her home life from newspaper articles published around the time of John Doherty's 80th birthday,[34] and obituaries published for Charlotte after her death in May 1924[35] and John's death in August 1929.[36] According to his Obituary, John Doherty's involvement in Irish Nationalist politics continued after the family arrived in England, and at one time he was asked to stand for an Irish parliamentary seat, but had to decline 'for business reasons'. This was probably related to the fact that he was reported as carrying on business in both Dublin and London at the time.

The same Obituary also provides evidence of his involvement in local public life from the outset of his arrival in England. John Doherty was reportedly a staunch Liberal, who was a member of the National Liberal Club for many years – having joined shortly after his arrival in England – becoming a Vice-President in 1930. As a result he was honoured by the Club on his 80th birthday with a lunch attended by many prominent Liberal political figures of the day. The lunch was presided over by the then Chairman, The Right

Honourable Earl Beauchamp, KG, KCMG, a senior establishment figure who, among his many roles, had been Lord Lieutenant of Gloucestershire since 1911, and who had carried the Sword of State at the coronation of King George V. The Earl was reported to have delivered a 'warm hearted and sincere' tribute to John Doherty in his speech.

Reading between the lines, however, provides further evidence of John Doherty's temperament and readiness to 'use his fists'. The Obituary records that early in his Liberal career he had been one of the '....foremost workers for Sir Sidney Pocock, J.P., when the latter nearly succeeded in capturing the seat for Liberalism, Sir Frederick Dixon Hartland being his Conservative opponent'. At one meeting during that election campaign, presided over by Mr Doherty, considerable heckling ensued, which was only stopped when Mr Doherty, 'having threatened to eject the interrupter, proceeded to take off his coat to suit the action to the word!'

John Doherty also served on the Teddington District Council and after making his presence felt on many local issues, was finally elected Chairman of the Council in 1906[36] He also served as a Justice of the Peace (JP) and deputy chairman of the Spelthorne Bench, for many years. He attended Justices' Meetings weekly from 1906 right up to his death in 1929[37]. The Justices were responsible for four committees on Prisons, Parliament, Riots and Licensing. In 1922 he was unanimously elected to the Standing Joint Committee and as Chairman of the

County Licensing Committee in December 1927 and 1928. During the whole period of his service as a JP the Minutes show he was responsible for local licensing issues covering public houses and off licences. His colleagues on the committee included Sir Sidney Pocock (Chairman), Sir George Metcalf, Lord Lucan and Sir Edward Nicholl.

John's Obituary described the quality of his judgements in this role as being informed by 'penetrating insight rather than judicial knowledge'. Further reading between the lines suggests that his colleagues considered he could be extremely partial in his judgements, particularly where speeding motorists were concerned, as he never travelled by car himself, disliking it as a form of transport. This was to be confirmed by an incident in the final year of his life in which John Doherty was knocked down by a 'speeding' motorist[38] when alighting from a tram outside his house. In giving evidence against the motorist his reply to the question as to whether he was a 'regular traveller' on the trams caused some laughter when he stated, 'I was until your client tried to finish me off'. The defendant was found guilty and his licence endorsed.

The Doherty household must have been a lively place where politics and the law dominated activities and friendships, and where networking and social functions connected to these activities saw many lively discussions. Prefiguring Norah's later suffragette activity it is interesting to note that between 1905 and 1922 there were three Liberal Prime Ministers in succession; Henry Campbell Bannerman (1905-1908); Herbert Asquith (1908-1916); and David Lloyd George (1916-1922). It was during the Asquith General Election campaign in 1910 that he announced that if returned to power he would enfranchise women with property. It was the breaking of this promise in November 1911 that enraged the WSPU who began their most extensive and final militant campaign, including window breaking, during which Asquith's home was attacked. Norah's rise to prominence within the WSPU from spring 1913 and her involvement in the militancy must have been a cause of some embarrassment/friction between her and John Doherty given his role as a leading liberal and longstanding Justice of the Peace on the Spelthorne Bench at that time.

Norah did not marry until she was 31. The marriage was to Charles Richard Dacre Fox, a wholesale stationery clerk aged 32 on 8 May 1909 in the Church of England Parish Church of Hampton in the County of Middlesex.[39] Norah's parents and her uncle Thomas Clarke all attended the wedding. As John Doherty had been running a printing business since his arrival in England, it is likely that Charles made the acquaintance of the Dohertys through business links. Charles was the eldest son of Richard Dacre Fox, a surgeon from Manchester. John Doherty presumably thought the son of a surgeon would be a suitable match for one of his daughters, although with Norah being 31, he may have been keen for any match to be made at all. Norah had little respect for doctors as will become clear, and she may not have been particularly impressed with her new father-in-law.

Richard Dacre Fox, born in 1847, had been trained in Medicine at Charing Cross Hospital in London.[40] Coming from a Derbyshire family probably explained why he returned closer to home to spend most of his career working in Manchester and Leeds in public medicine roles, including medical officer for Manchester Workhouse, surgeon to Manchester Police and Fire Brigade, surgeon to the Great Northern Railway, and chief medical officer for a number of other railway companies. These public roles brought him to attention in a number of local news reports; for example in 1871 it was reported in the Manchester Times[41] under the heading 'Baby Farming in Manchester' that he performed a post-mortem and gave expert medical evidence concerning a child's body found by policemen in a house search. He was also reported in the local press for his libel action against a company selling 'Mother Seigel's Curative Syrup', in which he was awarded damages of £1,000.[42] The company had distributed about 7.5 million copies of a pamphlet alleging that Mr Dacre Fox had '….so seriously blundered in treating the man Perrin that he had started the latter on the highway to the grave from which he had been rescued by the taking of Mother Siegel's Curative Syrup'.

Richard and his wife Mary Augusta Sacre had at least four children, Charles being the eldest. Although Richard is sometimes referred to as 'Mr Dacre Fox' in the press, his lineage clearly indicates that 'Dacre' was a middle name and not part of a double barrelled surname. Richard and Mary's other children were all known as 'Fox' and only Charles, being the first born, seems to have been given 'Dacre' as a middle name, after his father, whose own father was known simply as 'Richard Fox', born in 1821 in Yorkshire. Undoubtedly, 'Mrs Dacre Fox' sounded far more well-to-do than simply 'Mrs Fox', and whether it was initially on Charles' or Norah's insistence that 'Dacre' be employed as part of their surname, Norah never seems to have objected to being known as 'Mrs Dacre Fox'.

Charles and Norah set up home at 3 The Parade, Claygate, Surrey,[43] but the relationship, whatever it may have been built on, deteriorated quickly.

ALL THAT CROWD: DACRE FOX AND THE PANKHURSTS

SOCIETY WOMAN

Emmeline Pankhurst formed the WSPU in Manchester in 1903. Her three daughters (Christabel being the eldest, Sylvia and Adela) were involved in the movement from early on. The onset of militancy as a campaign tactic began in 1905 when Christabel Pankhurst and Annie Kenney were arrested and imprisoned in Manchester. The organisation began to adopt the slogans 'Votes for Women' and 'Deeds not Words', and in 1906, the WSPU moved its headquarters to London. Pugh[44] identifies this decision on the part of the Pankhursts as being 'shrewd in perceiving the advantages …….. in terms of funds as well as status'. In 1908 the militant tactics of the WSPU intensified following a demonstration in Hyde Park attended by 500,000 activists, while the first suffragette hunger strike took place in 1909, the year of Norah's marriage to Charles.

There is no evidence that Norah was a member of the WSPU in these early years around the time of her marriage, and while Norah may have begun to notice and sympathise with the cause at this time, her marriage at first prevented her joining such a renegade organisation. Pugh mistakenly identified Norah as being one of 37 well-to-do ladies making major subscriptions or donations to the WSPU during the period 1906-1914. The evidence Pugh cited for including Norah in this list was a Daily Graphic newspaper cutting from the Janie Allen Papers in the National Library of Scotland (the date is unknown, but thought to be between 1910 and 1915). The article is headed 'Financiers of Militancy – Society Women who gave to the cause'.[45] In it Mrs Dacre Fox is referred to as one of the prominent women with social standing and influence that the WSPU could rely on for support.

The article provides no specifics about Norah actually donating any money to the WSPU, but does indicate that Norah was well able to give the press the impression of being a 'society woman' with wealth and status even though this may not have been the case. The WSPU annual accounts 1908-1913 which were also cited by Pugh as his source for the list of 37 major subscribers[46] did not identify Norah as a subscriber or donator until the accounting period 1912-1913 in which she is recorded as having given the sum of one shilling, which, according to the rules of membership laid out in the Annual Reports, was the annual subscription fee.[47] It is also around this time that Norah's name began to appear regularly in the suffragette press, and it therefore seems likely that Norah joined the WSPU in 1912. An interview with Miss Grace

Roe in 1974 also confirms that Norah joined the organisation around this time along with a few other notable late arrivals.[48]

Norah rose quickly within the WSPU beginning her career as the Honourable Secretary of the Kingston and District Division.[49] Norah was required to organise local fundraising and branch meetings, and to report on branch activities in The Suffragette, the weekly publication of the WSPU. A typical weekly report shows the types of work required:

> *Helpers asked to be at Assembly Rooms two o'clock tomorrow (Saturday). Those who can come during morning earnestly asked to do so. Secretary will be there from 8.30 am. Refreshments or contributions should be taken to hall tomorrow morning as early as possible. Fruit and flowers for decoration still wanted. Fancy articles, home made sweets and cakes and contributions to White Elephant stall also welcome. Gratefully acknowledged contributions of articles : (list of names). Miss Fergus also thanked for presenting prize to Competition. The Misses Rayne and Miss Pearce welcomed as new members. Splendid cottage meeting West Molesey October 4, addressed by Mrs Cook. Every seat filled. Scotch Café same evening, when Mrs Cook again spoke. Mrs Beatty presided. Coronation Stone meeting address by Mrs Dacre Fox. Miss Stewart presided for first time. Members asked to note East End demonstration Victoria Park, and to keep November 10 free. There is still time for members to work hard for Dutch Market. Tickets must be sold in large numbers. (list of donations given). Hon Sec – Mrs Dacre Fox*

Clearly Norah had a busy role, organising fund raising activities such as jumble sales and Dutch Markets, selling tickets for fund raising events and organising speakers and attendees for weekly recruiting meetings. Entries in other weeks indicate that sheets were circulated asking for volunteers for demonstrations and sellers for The Suffragette for the coming week. In addition there was a role in recording and keeping account of all money collected and accounted for to headquarters.

Fitting with her 'society woman' status, Norah held regular 'At Home' events which were publicised in The Suffragette[50] and also sometimes in The Times.[51] This type of forum was adopted by the WSPU as a way of recruiting and fund raising.[52] In spite of the militant principles and activities of the WSPU, branch activities and 'At Home' events read much like the activities of the more sedate Women's Institute, which was formed in the UK in 1915 (when the WSPU and other suffrage organisations ended their campaigns) and was led by former suffragists Lady Denman and Grace Haddow.[53] The activities Norah was involved in, therefore, resembled a very much more respectable side of society than the militancy that the WSPU was associated with. The juxtaposition of respectability with militancy in the tactics of the WSPU is striking, and no doubt was appealing to Norah's wish for a place in society along with her fierce opinions, but it seems unlikely that her attempts at respectability would have washed with Charles who would have suffered intense embarrassment at Norah's activities.

When Norah began suffrage activities in 1912 she had been married to Charles Dacre Fox for three years and had no children. Charles and Norah believed that Norah was responsible for their childless marriage and the relationship must have been experiencing considerable difficulty by 1912. Norah's involvement in WSPU activity either came after the relationship had formally ended, or contributed directly to its final demise. The level of activity in which Norah became involved with the WSPU would have left her little time to devote to her marriage, and this would not have been welcomed by Charles, particularly as there would have been no small degree of shame to be a man with a wife who was not just infertile but also a suffragette.

What neither Norah nor Charles realised at the time was that it was Charles who was infertile. Charles and Norah never divorced, but according to his will, Charles eventually found another companion, Gladys Clara Dean, with whom he lived in a childless relationship. Charles' will for which probate was granted in February 1943 after his death in December 1942 read 'I give all my real and personal property of which I may die possessed unto my dear friend Gladys Clara Dean commonly known as 'Mrs GC Fox' as a very slight recognition of her devotion and constant care she has given me for many years'.[54] Norah also eventually found another companion and discovered to her horror that she was not infertile.

WORDS

By March 1913, Norah had been promoted to General Secretary of the WSPU[55] and became closely associated with the Pankhursts. As a woman in her 30s, Norah was an attractive lively woman who was said to have looked a lot like Christabel Pankhurst,[48] who was only two years Norah's junior. Norah was most highly prized by Emmeline and Christabel for her public speaking talents, and she used these when delivering speeches, chairing public meetings and acting as a press spokeswoman. Norah's speeches were rousing, defiant and often theatrical.

Norah's prolific public speaking activities in the WSPU stretched far beyond her own branch in Kingston. In one week in November 1912 she gave a talk every day at different venues in East London (Bethnal Green, Limehouse and Poplar).[49] Thereafter, she is recorded as giving regular talks in and around Kent, Sussex and London between two and five times a week.

Norah also chaired the WSPU weekly public meetings which were usually held at Knightsbridge Town Hall. Meetings were publicised in the Times and the press, and the public were encouraged to attend. There would usually be an invited speaker, and Norah, as General Secretary would report on national events and deliver press statements. Occasionally she delivered the main speaker address as well. Press reports were written and delivered for their propaganda value, and were no doubt aimed at presenting the leadership's message to their own membership as well as the public at large. Norah's weekly reports at the public meetings were printed in The Suffragette anonymised, though many of these statements appeared non-anonymised and attributed to her in The Times and other newspapers.

Norah had clearly been coached in the art of public speaking and delivered pointed speeches remarkably well. Although the WSPU provided training for its members in public speaking,[56] Norah joined the WSPU already having these skills. Norah was not just skilled in delivering speeches, but also in writing them. According to Grace Roe in an interview in 1974, Christabel Pankhurst would give Norah an idea or sentence on which to base a speech, and Norah would do the rest. Christabel was very impressed with Norah's speeches and praised their emotional expressiveness.[48] Norah's first speech as General Secretary, printed in The Suffragette, shows Norah's talent for spin:

The Self-Denial street sales of 1913 have beaten all records. Now that the strenuous days are ended, one can quietly look back on great things accomplished in spite of every effort which was made to discourage those engaged in this work of self sacrifice.

The Press, anxious to belittle and misrepresent the strength of the militant agitation, and to take away from the public sympathy and support, which is indisputable, has spent its time reporting only those incidents derogatory to the public, and none of those which go to show how the wind really blows.

Here we have one paper recording how women were mobbed when they ventured out with barrel organs, there another with large headlines suggesting rough handling of the women who were selling their wares in the streets. But what are the true facts of Self-Denial week? With the exception of a few incidents of the kind referred to in the papers, the public, without exception have responded in every direction to the indomitable courage of the women. Flower sellers have sold out almost before they had time to get settled at their various pitches. At Charing Cross a street flower seller has shown such interest in one of our women that the middle of the week had not been reached ere she had begged a badge from the member selling, and had proudly worn it ever since. Men and women stopping to buy a bunch of violets have time and again put down 1s or 2s 6d and refused change.

The collectors and sweet sellers record the same story. Our first question when they return to Lincoln's Inn House is, 'How are the crowds?' and the answer comes at once, 'Splendid!' The organ grinders, in spite of the rough handling recorded in the daily Press, have gone out each day making music and money at the same time. Collecting boxes have had to be opened daily as they had got too heavy to bear any more, and in many gold has been found.

One of the most noted Self-Denial weeks in our Union will be always that of 1913, and such experiences make the spirit of the WSPU all the stronger. They do to show not only those without, but also those within, the meaning and the unconquerable strength of the women's movement.[55]

The following week her report shows her talent for driving an impassioned and persuasive plea to the membership of the WSPU who were clearly afraid of taking on jobs that brought them into contact with the angry public or 'spiteful' Press:

General Secretary's Report – What every Suffragette can do.

Such wonderful results have attended the efforts recently made to increase the circulation of The Suffragette *that everyone will realise it only requires an army of sellers to reach the public at every point. Here is work that every Suffragette can do. Those who have been engaged in attending special functions to sell the paper bring back news that they meet with courtesy and interest everywhere. If members would but realise the amount of prejudice which* The Suffragette *is overcoming, why they would respond a thousandfold to the call for workers in this direction.*

There is so much misrepresentation at the present moment in the Press, not only of the Cause itself, but of the individual workers, that this scheme should do wonders to destroy the impressions created by the subsidised Press. Those who undertake the work should see that they dress themselves in their smartest clothes and make every effort to counteract the spiteful attempts commonly made by the Press not only to describe the deeds of Suffragettes as those of 'wild women,' but also to make Suffragettes themselves look the part.

Give a day or an hour

During this coming week a very special effort should be made by every member to give some time – a day, or even an hour, will be helpful as during Suffragette Week the sales must be enormously increased.

In various other directions help is also needed. The poster parades to advertise The Suffragette require helpers; the chalking parties need assistance, and, most important of all, members should concentrate on obtaining new regular subscribers. No member should let this week go by without adding at least six regular subscribers to our paper.

With regard to the display of posters, the extreme importance of this cannot be over-rated; for if readers will consider the extraordinary effect of a scheme of this kind carried out successfully, they will hasten to help with it.

No member of the WSPU will be able to say that she could not help during Suffragette week, for the variety of the schemes arranged make it open to everyone to do her share, if not in one way, then in another.[57]

The Suffragette newspaper is striking in terms of the extent of anonymity within it, both in terms of authors of articles, as well as the absence of names of women involved in the activities reported. While weekly militant activities were described in detail, no names of perpetrators were given and articles usually began with 'One Brave Lady this week appeared in court in …. on charges of…'. Authored articles were the exception and these tended to be written by leading figures who were beyond anonymity within the cause.

Christabel Pankhurst wrote the weekly editorial, always lengthy, printed on its own page, and signed. Other guest authors and leading public figures were invited to contribute under their own name, among them Dame Ethel Smyth. Norah evidently had the conviction and bravado to join those non-anonymous authors and named activists, and she revelled in her public association with the Pankhursts. But the majority of members clearly remained afraid of being identified with the cause, which was a significant hindrance to the WSPU.

Militant tactics would have been alien to the large majority of Edwardian women and would have required great courage to execute. Many would have feared the embarrassment that knowledge of their actions would cause their families. As a result, Harrison notes, 'Many suffragettes died without telling their story.[58] At the moment of militancy, militants are often so preoccupied with the world of action that they have little time (and perhaps also little talent or inclination) for sustained writing and thought. It would anyway be dangerous for them to preserve correspondence during the period of militancy itself; the police raided the WSPU headquarters more than once.' Mary Richardson when writing her autobiography Laugh a Defiance[59] many years later certainly adopted the same principle. None of her colleagues were identified by name, and her autobiography is written in the same anonymised style as that adopted in The Suffragette. Norah was notably different in this respect and although she never wrote an autobiography, she never shrank from reminding her associates in later life of her involvement in the militant suffragette campaign.

Norah became very close to Grace Roe, a fellow Irish woman in the inner circle of the Pankhursts, who was particularly close to Christabel Pankhurst and remained so all her life, being named executor of Christabel's estate when she died in 1958. According to Roe she had been identified by the Pankhursts to take over the position of WSPU Chief Organiser from Annie Kenney, in the event that she was arrested and imprisoned.[60] This event happened unexpectedly early in the spring of 1913 following a raid on the WSPU offices when Annie Kenney was indeed arrested and taken to prison. Grace Roe then began a period of high profile activity for the WSPU, which included responsibility for arranging Emily Wilding Davison's funeral following her death after throwing herself under the King's horse at Epsom.

Norah's friendship with Grace had begun sometime before the spring of 1913 after Grace was released from a period of imprisonment under the Cat and Mouse Act and Norah wrote asking how she could help. Grace and Norah became responsible for making up the middle page of The Suffragette together during which they enjoyed jokes, fun and laughter, especially when they had to do their work in hiding on some occasions in a flat in Earl's Court after a warrant was issued for Grace's arrest. Grace relied heavily on Norah, who 'played a big role for her' and recounted in particular the events of 1 May 1913 when the WSPU offices were raided and Norah helped her get out an edition of The Suffragette despite the authorities attempts to stop it being published.

Grace had gone to the WSPU offices to discuss the contingency plans for her promotion to Chief Organiser, when the raid began. All the chief office staff were targeted for arrest, including Rachel Barrett and Geraldine Lennox, the heads of the Editorial Department for The Suffragette. In the confusion Roe herself was not recognised as a WSPU official, managing to escape with many of the junior office staff, who also had the foresight to grab as much copy for the edition of The Suffragette to be published the next day that they could by stuffing it into their clothes and hiding it about their persons. Having left the WSPU headquarters and met elsewhere, the next problem facing Grace was how to get money and a substitute printer for The Suffragette. The money problem she solved by going to her bank and cashing in some personal bonds, while she delegated Norah and Joan Wickham to find a printer willing to publish.

Grace describes how, after obtaining £500 she went to the Westminster Committee Rooms where the WSPU had some alternative accommodation, arriving at the same time as Norah and Joan Wickham who emerged from a taxi with Mr Drew of the Victoria House Printing Company Limited who was willing to publish the 2 May edition of The Suffragette. Norah must have used her personal contacts in the printing industry gained through knowledge of her father's printing business to persuade Mr Drew to help the WSPU. During the next few hours they managed to put together eight pages of proof, and the printer took this and produced an edition that appeared on the streets the next day with the front page carrying the enlarged headline 'RAIDED'. Although the distribution of this edition of The Suffragette was severely restricted, its publication nevertheless caused a considerable furore amongst the authorities because they thought they had taken all necessary steps to ensure the publication would not be available for sale that week, but they had clearly not counted on the tenacity of Grace and her team and their determination to get the paper out.

Mr Drew was subsequently prosecuted for 'conspiring to incite violence' by printing the 2 May edition, and in all during this period the WSPU were forced to use several different printers. Mr Whitely, Manager of the National Labour Press Ltd (9 May edition) was also prosecuted for conspiring with the Pankhursts to incite members of the WSPU to violence. The editions of 16 May through 6 June were printed by J Edward Francis of Bream's Building Chancery Lane, but it was not until 13 June that Utopia Press took over weekly printing of The Suffragette and continued to do so from then on.

Norah reciprocated Grace's reliance on her and their closeness publicly, giving her fulsome praise during a speech she gave at Knightsbridge Hall in August 1914.[61] Evidently Norah used her talent for speaking both for the benefit of the organisation as well as for her own relationships:

I want also to couple my praises for my colleague, Miss Grace Roe, with those of the Chairman. I have been in close touch with her since the last raid, and I want to pay my tribute to her. If one is to be picked out of the galaxy of gems in this wonderful Union, I think, during the last year, the name of Grace Roe stands very prominent.

I could tell you things which perhaps none of you know, because I, being constantly with her, have seen it, how perhaps for some days she would have no food at all, working till two and three in the morning, and many times all night; going about her duties always with a light heart, always with her eyes fixed on the one thing, inspiring us who were fortunate enough to work under her. I wish I could convey to you what this great woman has been to us during that time.

I want to say that her trial and her fight is in keeping with all that she has shown us in the last year. I remember her saying to me, 'I am not going to rely upon speaking when I go into the dock. I am no speaker, but I shall take other ways.' And yet you see she was given a voice and words, eloquent words, to make her fight, and to bring that Court into disrepute and ridicule.

Many of Norah's weekly reports as General Secretary concerned Mrs Pankhurst and others who had been convicted of militancy, and who were out of prison on licence under the Cat and Mouse Act after hunger striking and being force fed. Mrs Pankhurst regularly breached the terms of her licence, but employed a bodyguard to protect her from re-arrest. Norah's speeches often goaded the authorities with blanket defiance on behalf of Mrs Pankhurst: 'She is not going to give herself up'.[62] 'If the bodyguard was to be bludgeoned by the police she could only say that they were going to stand no nonsense; they were not going to take any humbug from this Government or their paid servants'.[63] Norah also held no punches in her direct personal insults to the Prime Minister Lloyd George on behalf of Mrs Pankhurst stating in one speech: 'She did not suppose a more inaccurate, illogical, and crazy speech had ever been made by a Cabinet Minister'.

Norah was the defiant and unapologetic voice of the extreme activities of the WSPU. When three Suffragettes had 'thrashed' a Dr Forward outside Holloway Prison where he was the medical officer, Norah justified the assault, saying 'If Dr Forward was prepared to carry out the torture of women (forcible feeding) by Secretary McKenna's order, he must be prepared to take the consequences'.[64] Dr Forward and two other medical colleagues later sued the WSPU and a handful of named individuals, including Norah, for libel. The case was not concluded until 1916 by which time Norah and the Pankhursts were involved in the war effort, and did not appear in court to defend themselves. Dr Forward and his colleagues were awarded £750 damages.⁶⁵ Norah's disdain for doctors and the medical institution generally was no doubt fuelled by this episode and she would have revelled in the thought of the doctor being thrashed.

Norah also revelled in using dramatic theatre in her speeches. A favourite tactic she employed at public meetings to demonstrate the determination of the movement to confront the authorities, was by holding up copies of individual prisoner licences issued under the Cat and Mouse Act and displaying contempt for them. On several occasions she dramatically tore a licence in half on the platform at Knightsbridge Hall.⁶² Another such theatrical performance was reported in Times as follows:

> *Miss Kenney was conveyed to the meeting in a horse ambulance; and she was borne into the meeting on a stretcher, which was raised to the platform and placed on two chairs. She raised her right hand and fluttered a handkerchief and, covered with blankets, lay motionless watching the audience. Later, her licence under the 'Cat and Mouse' Act was offered for sale. Mrs Dacre Fox stated that an offer of £15 had already been received for it, and the next was one of £20, then £25 was bid, and at this price it was sold. Soon afterwards Miss Kenney was taken back to the ambulance. Detectives were present, but no attempt was made to rearrest Miss Kenney, who licence had expired.*⁶⁶

Violent scuffles with police became a regular feature at suffragette meetings where Christabel Pankhurst or

Annie Kenney would appear to speak in breach of their Cat and Mouse licences. Norah never wasted an opportunity to criticise and highlight the effects of this violence, as well as ensuring that WSPU funds benefited from it, on one occasion holding an auction for 'three relics' of just such a fight with police. Two broken hats and a walking stick ended up swelling funds by the best part of £7 or so.[67]

Deeds

Norah was not just a spokeswoman for the WSPU; her fiery dramatics on stage being matched by her defiant behaviour. Norah was imprisoned three times in Holloway Prison along with her WSPU colleagues and was subjected to forcible feeding.

The official name of what has become known as the 'Cat and Mouse Act' was the Prisoners Temporary Discharge for Ill Health Act 1913. This Act was passed in direct response to women's hunger striking while in prison for militant suffrage activity. The Act made hunger strikes legal and allowed for women to be released from prison on licence as soon as they became ill, while at the same time allowing the authorities to re-arrest the women if they contravened the terms of their licence. As part of this process women would be force fed. Lady

Constance Lytton described her experience of being force fed in 1910:

> *[The doctor] put down my throat a tube which seemed to me much too wide and was something like four feet in length. The irritation of the tube was excessive. I choked the moment it touched my throat until it had got down. Then the food was poured in quickly; it made me sick a few seconds after it was down and the action of the sickness made my body and legs double up, but the wardresses instantly pressed back my head and the doctor leant on my knees. The horror of it was more than I can describe. I was sick over the doctor and wardresses, and it seemed a long time before they took the tube out. As the doctor left me he gave me a slap on the cheek, not violently, but as it were, to express his contemptuous disapproval.*

Norah became actively involved in a campaign to expose the horrors of force feeding, and force the government to end its use on suffragettes. The conduct of this campaign saw Norah writing to or leading deputations to many prominent churchmen. The Bishop of Winchester, the Archbishop of Canterbury and the Bishop of London were all targeted, followed by the Archbishop of York and the Bishops of Croydon, Lewes, Islington and Stepney. Many churchmen were sympathetic to the women's movement, and in 1913 a number of clergymen had marched to Downing Street to protest against the Cat and Mouse Act, and also held a meeting in December 1913 in Queen's Hall, London, to protest against forcible feeding.[68] The WSPU may therefore have hoped to win support from the Church for their wider cause of suffrage by pressing on the issue of forcible feeding. The Church, when pressed, however, chose not to be drawn into a battle between the WSPU and the authorities, and clung to a party line that militancy was a precursor to forcible feeding and militancy was against the will of God, therefore the Church could not act against forcible feeding.

Norah led a band of suffragettes to the Archbishop of Canterbury on 29 January 1914:

> *The band of militant suffragettes who besieged the Archbishop of Canterbury in Lambeth Palace today and eventually forced him to capitulate was headed by Mrs Dacre Fox. It took them over an hour to obtain admission to the old palace on the bank of the Thames. They declined to listen to any attempt on the part of the inmates to temporize, and finally, seeing the futility of trying to escape from his obdurate blockaders, the Archbishop allowed Mrs Dacre Fox to enter.*[69]

Norah's report of her interview was printed in The Suffragette:

> *I told him that I did not wish on this occasion to discuss Woman Suffrage or militant methods, that each person had his or her opinion on this important question, but upon the matter on which I desired to see him there could be only one opinion. I explained that our reason for approaching him was his position as head of the Established Church in this country.*

He then asked me what I wanted him to do. I said that we wanted him to take action at once, and that the only thing for him to do if he wanted to get at the true state of affairs was to go to Holloway and investigate the whole matter, seeing, if necessary, the operation carried out, and the women struggling, and the whole fight in the cell.

I also told him that the point at issue was whether he thought that under certain conditions torture was justifiable if he thought that his course was clear.

He then asked me again what it was I wished him to do, and I said that I wanted him to tell me that he was prepared to go forward in this matter. He said that he could not be pressed, and that the only thing he could promise was that he would give the matter his deep consideration. I pointed out that while he was doing this, women were being tortured in prison, and that it was a matter of life and death. He said he quite realised the sincerity of those who felt this matter so strongly; indeed, he had, as I probably knew, intimate connections engaged in the work. I still asked him if he was prepared to do anything, and he again gave me the same answer.

I expressed myself as profoundly dissatisfied with his answer, and I added, on behalf of the deputation, that we considered his refusal to help us as absolutely contrary to the spirit of Christianity. I then withdrew.

Before I left I gave him a copy of Miss Pankhurst's book, and asked him to read it. He said he would have pleasure in doing so.[70]

To the Knightsbridge Hall audience that week, Norah gave a much more dramatic and derogatory account of the meeting:

'Rotter!' Cry Militants

The only feeling experienced by Mrs Dacre Fox, a suffragette leader, while she was interviewing the Archbishop of Canterbury... was 'utter contempt'... Mrs Dacre Fox said that the Archbishop's Chaplin was 'a pitiable object, trembling and with chattering teeth'.[70]

I can only say that as I sat looking at that old man, the feeling which was uppermost in my mind was that of contempt....I wondered if Calvary had almost been in vain.[68]

The Bishop of London became the next target of the WSPU campaign. The Bishop of London, the Right Reverend Arthur Foley Winnington Ingram, became involved because he went to Holloway on two occasions to visit militant Suffragettes under detention. Following a WSPU deputation to the Bishop of London, lead by Mrs Diplock, he arranged to visit Holloway to see Miss Rachel Peace, whom it was claimed was in poor health as a result of forcible feeding. A report had been made by a fellow prisoner Miss Ansell, who, after her release, reported that she had heard Miss Peace being force fed accompanied by 'a shriek of pain, uncontrollable, terrible pain, and then low moans, heart-breaking'.

Following his visit to Holloway the Bishop of London wrote to Mrs Diplock indicating that he had investigated the matter fully. The Bishop's response to her was published in The Morning Post stating that having interviewed both Miss Peace and the prison authorities, he had found Miss Peace well and comfortable in a large cell showing no 'signs of emaciation or distress'.[71] The Bishop ended his letter by stating, 'I have no hesitation in saying that if Miss Ansell heard shrieks they could not have been uttered by Miss Peace........and ......the fears which you express to me with regard to her condition are not borne out by the facts of the case.' The WSPU realised that the Bishop of London had already been in communication with the Archbishop of Canterbury on this matter prior to his interview with Norah and that together, they had decided to back the authorities.

The WSPU were 'incensed' by the Bishop's dismissal of ill treatment of Suffragette prisoners, and sent a group of suffragettes to Golders Green, where he was conducting a consecration service, to create a disturbance.[72] Mrs Diplock replied to the Bishop's letter and published a copy in The Morning Post. Norah also sent a letter to the Bishop which was published in the Post:

The Bishop of London in 'Blinkers'

The whole truth of the matter is that, like others, you have allowed the Government and the prison officials to hoodwink you. It is obviously their business so to do. The Home Office agrees to an investigation, and at the same time makes it of no avail, by putting blinkers on the investigators. A whitewash brush, my Lord Bishop, has been placed in your hand by the authorities, in order that the public shall still remain in ignorance of the diabolical methods used by the Government in their desire to terrorise the militant women. The deputation which waited upon you on Monday was earnest in urging you to insist upon seeing for yourself the operation of forcible feeding. We are of opinion that had you strongly persisted you could have wrung from them the permission to be present. Obviously, in the circumstances, your investigation of the horrors of forcible feeding was no investigation at all…..

…It is clear, then, that in the case of the Suffragists the Home Secretary is not punishing them for what they have done, but is inflicting, or threatens to inflict this torture upon them to prevent them doing in the future what they believe to be their duty [referring to an offer to release Miss Peace if she agrees to cease suffragist activity]. An endeavour to force a recantation of principle is, and always has been, the essence of torture.[73]

Whether this raised level of rhetoric from the WSPU had any impact on him, or whether other factors were at play, the Bishop of London did in fact decide to make a second visit to Holloway. A WSPU deputation led by Miss Dunlop urged him to visit two more prisoners, Miss Marian and Miss Phyllis Brady, which he did. He makes a full report of his visit, again published in the Post under the heading 'Bishop of London's Second Visit to Holloway – The Screams Explained'.[74] In this letter the Bishop asserts that he could not get a permit to witness force feeding, but only to visit specified women prisoners for interview purposes. Both times he had been to Holloway unannounced, and as with his visit to Miss Peace, he had found the prisoners well. He had discussed force feeding with Miss Marian and Miss Brady. Miss Marian had indicated that her screaming during force feeding constituted a form of protest, while Miss Brady believed silence was a more appropriate way of protesting. The Bishop insisted that this explained the screams reported to him as having been heard by Miss Ansell. The Bishop also insisted that he believed that any force feeding carried out was done 'in the kindest possible spirit'. The Bishop made it plain that he regarded militancy as something of which he strongly disapproved and ended his letter by stating 'Many of you are actuated by religious motives, but you will forgive my reminding you that God's will can only be done in God's way.' Miss Phyllis Brady, through her solicitor, repudiated the Bishop's statements.[75]

Norah's Knightsbridge speech the next week[76] takes up the Bishop's accusation that the militants were failing in their Christian duties. This clearly incensed Norah and she makes her boldest accusation yet against the Church, damning the two Bishops to the judgment of God, drawing parallels with Christ's crucifixion at the hands of Pontius Pilate:

The Church Stands Indicted Before the Almighty

I want to start with the part of the letter which refers to the will of God. We are acting in accordance with the will of God (Applause). That banner which faces me says 'Resistance to tyranny is obedience to God.' And I have to say to the Bishop of London that he has allied himself with the Archbishop of Canterbury on the side of those who are prepared to go on torturing women. I want also to say that we charge the Church as a whole with the same crime. We know that there are individual clergymen who have stood in the face of all, side by side, with the right and with the just: and those men we appreciate and honour; but the Church as a whole stands indicted before this judgment of the Almighty, while it stands today watching the torture of those women in Holloway Prison.

Let the Bishop be Forcibly Fed

In answer to the Bishop's letter, I call upon him to come to this hall next Monday afternoon and be forcibly fed before this audience, so that in a practical manner he can give voice to the faith that is in him. There is no other possible way to getting to the bottom of this matter. He has refused to see the thing in operation himself. He has gone to the prison, and instead of asking Miss Marian and Miss Phyllis Brady whether there was truth in the statements which they have sent out to us, he has talked with them about Votes for Women and militancy, and tried to tempt them, as he did Miss Peace, with an offer to set them free, if they will give up their convictions. I repeat again that the Bishop of London is acting as an ally of this

Government, and cannot be considered an impartial judge in this issue.

We have given the Bishop and the Archbishop every chance to come out and take a strong line. They have failed, and to them punishment will come. Be sure that the day is not far off, that it is absolutely sure that the time will come, and at no distant date, when those men will get their reward, the reward of him who calls 'Crucify, crucify'.[76]

The following week Norah reported to the WSPU weekly meeting that Miss Phyllis Brady had been drugged by the prison authorities before her interview with the Bishop of London in Holloway jail,[77] noting that the WSPU intended to bring this 'grave scandal' to the 'attention of Parliament'. According to the WSPU, Miss Brady had provided a full account of her drugging, backed up by evidence from her doctor.[78]

Further deputations were sent to see other leading churchmen. Fifty-one women from the Yorkshire branch of the WSPU, accompanied by Norah, visited London to brief the Archbishop of York on the facts of forcible feeding.[79] Norah indicated that neither she nor the delegation had been impressed with the Archbishop's attitude to the matter. Other deputations led by Norah were then sent to the Bishops of Lewes and Croydon in February[80] and the Bishops of Islington and Stepney in March.[81] Norah gave long reports in The Suffragette of her interviews and arguments made to the Bishops, to whom she spoke of forcible feeding as tantamount to murder:

> *I at once went into the matter of forcible feeding, describing at some length the physical effects given by Dr Cowen on Monday, and showing the dangers of forcibly feeding resisting the people with a view to keeping them in health. Again and again I pointed out to him that the Government were not carrying out the law, because they were not making their prisoners serve the sentences imposed upon them – they were only prolonging the torture, and had in every case of a long sentence to liberate the woman or kill her. This punishment, carried out to a logical conclusion, would be murder.*

It appears that the WSPU did not persuade any of the Bishops they approached to come out against forcible feeding. All the Bishops are reported as colluding with each other and with the authorities, claiming that militancy was against God's will and that forcible feeding was not an unreasonable approach to dealing with the imprisoned militants. Prefiguring her contribution to the campaign against Sir Edward Carson, Norah reportedly asked the Bishop if the same policy would apply to Ulster militancy. The Bishop apparently responded that the WSPU situation was different, and that the 'Ulster rebels had created a situation which the Government had to accept'. Norah replied, 'This is a direct incitement to militancy. We are to create a situation which is such a terrible menace that the Government must yield, then you will support us?' The Bishop did not give way.

Front Page, The Suffragette, 13 February 1913

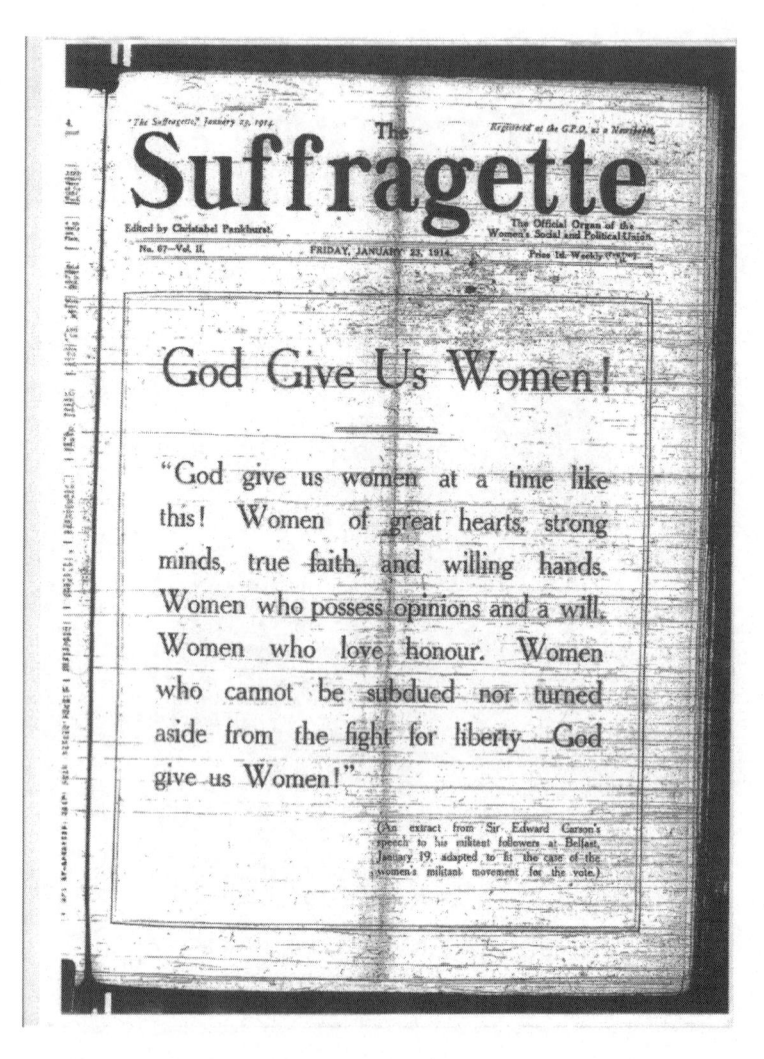

Front Page, The Suffragette, 23 January 1914

ULSTER CONNECTIONS

A Home Rule Bill for Ireland had first been put forward in 1886 by the Liberal Prime Minister William Gladstone who had been negotiating with the Irish nationalist leader Charles Stuart Parnell. The Bill was opposed by Conservatives and many Liberals also defected, leading to its defeat. It was also opposed by the Protestants of Ulster who were beginning to organise against the nationalist threat. Parnell and Gladstone attempted to placate Ulster and both were adamant that Home Rule for Ireland should mean a united Ireland. It was in this context in 1888 that Norah had been brought to England by her father who was a firm supporter of Parnell. Parnell died in 1891 in disgrace following humiliating revelations about his long term affair with Katherine O'Shea, but the nationalist cause continued and a second Home Rule Bill was put forward in 1893. It was again defeated, but the Orangemen of Ulster continued to organise and agitate against the Home Rule movement, supported by the Conservative Party in England.

Sir Edward Carson, a wealthy Ulster landowner, had founded the Ulster Unionist Party in 1905, and as such became the voice of Ulster Protestantism in the English Parliament. As an Irish and British barrister, judge, politician and leader of the Irish Unionist Alliance and Ulster Unionist Party between 1910 and 1921, he held numerous positions in the Cabinet of the United Kingdom and served as a Lord of Appeal in Ordinary. Prior to that in 1877 Carson had been called to the Irish Bar at King's Inns, and as a barrister he had been appointed Queen's Counsel in 1889. Perhaps most famously in 1895, he was engaged by the Marquess of Queensberry to lead his defence against Oscar Wilde's libel action.

As a third Home Rule Bill began to look increasingly likely to succeed in 1912, Lord Carson, as leader of the Ulstermen opposed to the Bill, began to demand an amendment granting the exclusion of the Ulster counties from its operation. The Bill was, however, passed in 1912, unamended, leading to the unleashing of the militancy which had been gathering and arming itself in the counties of Ulster. In 1913 the Ulster Volunteer Force was founded, recruiting men through the Orange Lodges. On 19 January 1914 Sir Edward Carson made a speech in Belfast followed by a press statement on 21 February that if Ireland was granted Home Rule with a parliament in Dublin, they would establish a rival parliament in Ulster. Sir Edward Carson openly announced that gun-running was already underway and that men were being trained for this eventuality.

Norah never declared herself in support of Irish Nationalism or referred much to the troubles in Ireland. However, the strategic decision by the WSPU leadership to bring the issue of militancy to the fore by attacking the Ulster Unionists and drawing direct parallels between their militancy and suffragette militancy put Norah on ground she understood well, probably arising out of an affinity for Irish Nationalism shared with her father. Carson's announcement of the beginning of Ulster militancy was a red rag to a bull for Norah and the WSPU.

Following Carson's open declaration of militancy, the WSPU saw an opportunity to undermine the government's treatment of the suffragettes, particularly with regard to force feeding. To emphasise the parallels between the WSPU and Ulster, The Suffragette[82] carried on its front page a bowdlerised extract from Carson's speech, replacing 'men' for 'women': 'God give us women at a time like this! Women of great hearts, strong minds, true faith, and willing hands. Women who possess opinions and a will. Women who love honour. Women who cannot be subdued nor turned aside from the fight for liberty – God give us Women!' The WSPU campaign set out to draw parallels between Ulster and WSPU militancy, and expose the government's unequal treatment of them. They also sought to expose the leaders of Ulster Unionism and to drive out evidence of hypocrisy in their manifesto.

Members of The Ulster Women's WSPU arrived in London in March 1914 to lobby Carson,[83] their deputation being led by Flora Drummond. The Ulster women wanted Carson to refuse to accept any settlement of the Home Rule question that did not guarantee women full citizenship rights, including the vote. Carson refused to receive the delegation, and so they decided to lay siege to his London home by camping on his doorstep. The Suffragette announced, 'Sir Edward Carson Declares War on Women – The Siege of Eaton Square'.[84]

Carson, being actively and publicly engaged in supporting gun running and the development of a fighting force, was identified and portrayed in The Suffragette as a traitor, promoting the use of physical violence to achieve the ends of his Ulster Unionist allies, but who was never arrested or prosecuted by the British authorities for doing so. The WSPU compared this with their own 'mild' form of militancy, which they claimed was never designed to kill or maim people, only to attack property or other inanimate targets.

During March and April 1914, Norah corresponded with HM Office of Works to seek permission for a WSPU demonstration in Hyde Park, printing the correspondence in full in The Suffragette. Norah also turned up in person at Scotland Yard to pursue the matter, complaining of delays and prevarication:

HM Office of Works

Storeys Gate SW
March 28, 1914

Dear Sir, – We have your letter which is entirely unsatisfactory, and we notice from an announcement in the Press that the Government have already given permission for a meeting to be held in Hyde Park on Saturday next by the advocates of the policy of violence and bloodshed in Ulster.

There can therefore be no objection to a WSPU meeting which does not apply even more strongly for the meeting of Ulster militants next Saturday.

We therefore shall decline to accept any refusal of our application to hold meetings in Hyde Park. We regard the delay in according to our request as a grave discourtesy and as tantamount to a refusal of our request.

We therefore wish to say that if we do not receive, by 12 o'clock today, a definite permission to hold meetings in Hyde Park, we shall send to the newspapers an announcement of a meeting to be held by the WSPU in Hyde Park next Saturday afternoon at the same time as the Ulster demonstration.

Yours faithfully, Norah Dacre Fox[85]

The permit was finally refused by the authorities on the grounds that the WSPU had asked for a vehicle for use as a speaker's platform during the rally, and vehicles were not allowed to be taken over the grass. Permission to demonstrate on the same day having been granted to Carson's Ulstermen, provided fodder for more WSPU headlines about the unequal treatment of WSPU and Ulster militants: 'As the advocates of violence and bloodshed in Ulster are permitted to have proper facilities for holding their meeting, the WSPU regard the refusal of similar facilities to them as a further attempt on the part of the Government to coerce militant women, while conciliating militant men'.[85]

The WSPU had in the past been granted permission to hold demonstrations in Hyde Park, and the organisers of the WSPU would have been familiar with the process involved and the criteria they would need to meet to ensure the legality of the demonstration. This situation may, therefore, have been engineered by Norah to draw attention to the Ulster parallel. There is no reason to believe that the Commissioner of Works had suddenly lost objectivity towards the WSPU, and it seems likely that the objection made to the demonstration was a simple matter of following rules. Whether engineered or not, however, Norah, along with Flora Drummond now cranked up their rhetoric towards the Ulstermen and the government so far that the authorities were forced to move against them.

Militants and the Police – Summonses against Mrs Drummond and Mrs Dacre Fox

At the instance of the Commissioner of Police summonses have been granted by Mr Horace Smith at Westminster Police Court, for hearing on Thursday next, against Mrs Flora Drummond and Mrs Dacre Fox for using language at meetings at Knightsbridge, Chelsea Town Hall, Clapham, and other places, 'openly and deliberately advocating acts of militancy and violence.'

> *The defendants are required to show cause why they should not be ordered to enter into their recognisances and find sureties for future good behaviour.*[86]

As well as issuing summonses to Norah and Flora Drummond, a writ was issued against the printers of The Suffragette.[87] The reasons given for were that that this particular edition did not properly indicate that it had been printed by The Victoria House Publishing Co Ltd, and that it contained inciting material. According to The Suffragette on 15 May 1914, the case of the writ '....is one of very great importance from the point of view of the Press and country and of the entire printing trade. The Government have not yet instituted proceedings against the Unionist newspapers which have published incitement to militancy in Ulster'.[88] The publisher Sydney Drew was later convicted and sentenced to two months in jail.

The Suffragette did not shrink from the campaign however, directing yet more defiance directly at Ministers:

> *Mr Bonar Law [the Leader of the Conservative Party] has declared that in their opposition to Home Rule the Unionist Party will not be guided by the considerations and restrained by the bonds that would influence them in any ordinary political struggle but will use any means and whatever means seem likely to be the most effective, and that Ulster will be justified in resisting Home Rule by force. Mr Bonar Law has further said: 'We are told that it is monstrous that we, the*

> *Constitutional Party, should countenance resistance. What else can we do?' Ulster will fight, he says, 'as all great peoples have fought for their rights.' Sir Edward Carson long since announced that he intended to 'break every law that is possible' and that Ulster would 'meet the Home Rule Bill by force'. Informed that his policy was illegal, Sir Edward Carson has replied: 'Of course it is. Drilling is illegal, volunteers are illegal. The Government know they are illegal and the Government dare not interfere with what is illegal. Therefore do not be afraid of illegalities!' Applauding the warlike preparations for defiance which his supporters in Ireland are making, Sir Edward Carson said: 'With all my heart I commend that defiance to you.' No fair minded person can compare the speeches of Mrs Dacre Fox and General Drummond with the speeches of the Unionist leaders without realising anew how infamous is the Government's policy of coercing women while licensing the law breaking of men.*[89]

The Suffragette is also sneering about police methods: 'Serving the Summons on Mrs Dacre Fox – Farcical Proceedings' is the way it describes Scotland Yard's method of delivering the summons on a train platform as Norah returned from a holiday: 'Passengers travelling by the train and people waiting on the platform were much astonished by the extraordinary proceedings and of the caution and evident anxiety displayed by the Scotland Yard men'.[90]

Norah and Flora Drummond were due to appear in court to answer the summonses on Thursday 14 May 1914. Instead of attending court, Flora besieged the home of Lord Carson, while Norah did the same at the home of the 5th Marquis of Lansdowne in Berkeley Square. The Marquis had been chosen for this honour by the WSPU because of his position in the establishment not only as a politician and Irish peer, but because of his alignment with Lord Carson on the Ulster question. Again this was a significant figure in the political establishment who had served as Governor General of Canada, Viceroy of India, Secretary of State for War, and Secretary of State for Foreign Affairs, holding senior positions in both Liberal Party and Conservative Party governments during his career.

Norah was reported to have taken her night attire with her to Landsdowne's doorstep, hoping to gain lodging for the night. By the afternoon, she had 'given up hope of attaining a lodging, as the night attire she had brought with her in the morning was taken away by a friend in the course of the afternoon'.[91]

Suffragists Sanctuary – Siege of Houses of Unionist Leaders

The town houses both of Lord Lansdowne and Sir Edward Carson were 'picketed' yesterday by suffragists in order to emphasize their contention that the women's militancy is no worse than that of the Ulster leaders. The principal demonstrators were Mrs Dacre Fox and Mrs Drummond, who had been summoned to appear before the Westminster Magistrate later in the day on a charge of making inciting speeches. Neither appeared, and consequently later in the afternoon both were arrested.

Mrs Dacre Fox accompanied by two sympathizers, drove up in a motor-car to Lansdowne House, in Berkeley Square, shortly before 9 o'clock, and leaving one of her companions in the car Mrs Fox and the other entered the grounds and sent in a message to Lord Lansdowne. She explained to a Press representative that she had been summoned to appear in the afternoon for making inciting speeches and as Lord Lansdowne had also been making inciting speeches, yet seemed to be perfectly safe from interference, she thought she had better be with him so that if they took her they could take both. Shortly before 10 Mrs Dacre Fox and her friend were removed from the grounds by the police. They then began to ring and knock at the gates, until at last the police interfered.

Mrs Dacre Fox said she had not been successful in seeing Lord Lansdowne, but in reply to their message he had sent out a letter, which she preferred for the present not to make public.

At 10 minutes to 11 the police arrested Mrs Dacre Fox and took her to Vine Street Police Station…

….Dacre Fox, accompanied by two young supporters, had returned to Lansdowne House shortly before 2.30. A little later Lord Lansdowne walked out, but neither Mrs Dacre Fox nor her companions made any attempt to speak to him. Mrs Dacre Fox sat quietly reading on a camp-stool until 5.20, when Detective-Inspector Buckley, of the Special Branch at Scotland Yard, arrested her on the Westminster Magistrate's warrant.

According to an account of this incident given when Norah's suffragette medal came up for sale in 2006[92] the text of the letter that Norah delivered to Lord Lansdowne stated that 'a militant had come to another militant to shelter from arrest, thinking it the safest place they could come to' because, both Sir Edward Carson and Lord Lansdowne, 'had been enabled to go scot free'. Flora Drummond's letter to Lord Carson was the same, but while Norah's letter was described as being 'sent in', Mrs Drummond's letter appears to have been accompanied by 'documents containing militant quotations from his own speeches' thrown into his hall when police constables attempted to stop her talking to him as he emerged from the house. Lord Lansdowne's reply to Norah from his Secretary apparently stated, 'I am to say that it is impossible for him to allow you to take refuge in his house, in which, moreover, you would obviously still be within reach of the law. Lord Lansdowne has not seen the speeches which have led to proceedings taken against you. As to his own conduct, should it at any time render him liable to prosecution, he would certainly, if required to, appear before a magistrate, and not decline to do so'.

In the meantime, at the Police Court, where some confusion reigned because Norah and Mrs Drummond had not answered their summonses, warrants were issued for their arrests.

Police Court Application

At Westminster Police Court Mrs Drummond and Mrs Dacre Fox were summoned by the Commissioner of Police to show cause why they should not enter into recognisances and find sureties for using language calculated to provoke a breach of the peace.

The defendants did not appear when called, and Mr Muskett applied for warrants for their arrest....With regard to Mrs Dacre Fox, Mr Muskett went on to say that he suggested that her absence was due to part of a scheme by which she managed to get herself arrested for knocking at the door of Lord Lansdowne's house in Berkeley Square. This intentional manoeuvre had not been very successful. On learning that she was in custody at Vine Street Police Station, on Mr Muskett's instructions and with the concurrence of the learned magistrate at Marlborough Street Police Court, she was released from custody with directions that she was to appear before Mr Mead next day. Mr Horace Smith granted the warrants.[93]

Flora Drummond and Norah appeared in court the following day. The Suffragette depicts the court hearing as a heroic victory for the WSPU and Mrs Dacre Fox, in spite of the two receiving imprisonment:

The case of Mrs Dacre Fox was taken first. Immediately on entering the dock, she began to speak. 'I am not going to take any notice of these proceedings,' she said, 'you know that the whole thing is a farce, and that before we women come into the dock, you have got the rope round our necks.'

The Real Incitement

'If I am charged with making inciting speeches, why are not Sir Edward Carson and Lord Lansdowne and Mr Bonar Law standing beside me – these men who are guilty of incitement to take human life?' I was arrested on the doorstep of a man who has made worse incitements than I have made. I shall do exactly what my conscience tells me to do; if I want to go to prison I shall go; if I want to stay outside prison, I shall stay outside. It is an impossibility to make me give my consent to those things with which I do not agree.

I am here, a woman, standing among men who have no sense of justice, who belong to a sex which has exploited women from the beginning, exploited them economically, politically and sexually. You talk about incitement. I tell you the incitement comes from such men as you who are prepared to let these things go on. That is the incitement which has made women like us, women of exemplary character and life, come to the police-court, and tell you what we think.

I want to say this to you: I am going to make women rise up in any possible way. I am going to tell them that at the bottom is the sex problem, and that with men like this man Muskett, and McKenna, and the rest of the Government, at the bottom of their fear of women is the fear that women will not allow these things to go on.

Why Do You Not Prosecute These Men?

I want to know why women like us should be standing in this police-court today, when scoundrels are allowed to go through the country destroying the minds and bodies of little children. Why do you not prosecute these men? Why should you prosecute us women, whose only crime is that we stand for the downtrodden, sexually, economically, and politically? The whole thing is a travesty and a farce; it has become a public scandal. You are the laughing-stock of the world.'

Mr Muskett apparently tried to say something at this juncture, for Mrs Dacre Fox broke off, 'I don't want to hear anything you have to say. Be quiet.'

Mrs Dacre Fox continued to speak until the end of the case. The proceedings were so inaudible that when she left the dock everyone in the court was under the impression that she was going to be recalled later, and no one realised that she had already been sentenced.[94]

Norah was sentenced to one month imprisonment in Holloway where she began a hunger and thirst strike immediately. On sentencing, the prisoners refused to cooperate and when attempts were made to remove them to the cells they became so violent that four policemen were needed to remove them from the prisoner's enclosure. Even then they were removed from the court 'screaming and shrieking'.[95]

This whole incident was of sufficient concern that it was raised in the House of Commons by Mr Keir Hardie[92] who 'asked why proceedings had been initiated against Mrs. Drummond and Mrs. Dacre Fox for advocating acts of militancy and violence whilst no similar proceedings are contemplated against those Privy Counsellors, King's Counsel, and Army Officials who have been advocating a like policy in Ulster'. Mr. Hardie went on to say that he 'wondered if the advocacy of enfranchisement is a greater crime than advocating an armed rebellion against the State'. Apparently Minister McKenna replied by saying that 'such cases were sub judice, but it is the advocacy of arson and outrage that is the crime, not the advocacy of enfranchisement' that was the reason for the arrests. I suspect it is possible to imagine in what sarcastic and unflinching language Norah's response to such a duplicitous response would have been.

Norah had taken bold issue with the Protestant Church in both her campaigns. Norah clearly felt strongly about her Christian beliefs and was incensed at the Bishop of London's accusation that she was acting against God's will. Norah's experiences with the Established church leaders in England and the leading Protestants in Ulster may well be partly responsible for her loss of faith. We do not know when she lost her faith, but she was a self-declared atheist in the 1950s and probably so from as early as the 1930s. Certainly her writings and speeches during that time have lost the references to Christianity so prevalent in her suffragette campaign.

STONE WALLS

Norah was released from Holloway on 19 May 1914 on licence having been on hunger and thirst strike for five days.[96] During her imprisonment, Norah defiantly refused to undress or wash, and lay on her bed refusing to move. The only time she did do anything was to get up and break her cell windows, earning her three days solitary confinement on bread and water, which she was refusing anyway because she was on a hunger and thirst strike.[97]

After her release, Norah took up her place as Chair at Knightsbridge Hall as usual:

> *Mrs Dacre Fox who, in spite of a fine speech she made last Monday at the Knightsbridge Hall, is still far from well, has gone to the seaside. She is impatient to recover enough strength to enable her once more to join issues with the Government.*[98]

In that 'fine speech', along with her eloquent comments on 'incitement' and her praise of Miss Grace

Roe seen earlier, she speaks gravely of her prison experiences:

> *I had gone into prison for the first time, knowing nothing of it. I shall never forget the atmosphere of the place. For us Suffragettes, what does it matter? Wherever we are our surroundings touch us not at all; but it was the other women; the ordinary prisoners, it was the way those women are spoken to. It was the look in the eyes of the prisoner who came to wait in my cell, that frightened, hunted look!*

The Prison Atmosphere

> *Here in the 20th century men can still conceive that this is civilisation and they are prepared to go on with the present system, which no words can describe. Whoever gets into that prison, perhaps people not all bad, are likely to be turned out dangerous criminals.*
>
> *So far as I am concerned, I remember the words of Ernest Jones the Chartist. He said, 'I went into prison a Chartist. I came out a revolutionary.' I went into prison a Militant Suffragette. I came out fifty militants rolled into one.*
>
> *I learnt a verse out of the Bible when I was in prison, which I am going to repeat to you this afternoon. St Paul says to the Romans: 'I am persuaded that neither life nor death, neither angels nor powers, nor principalities, nor things present, nor things to come, nor height nor depth, nor any other creature, can separate us from that which we believe to be right.'*

On returning from the seaside, Norah set out to be rearrested. She wrote to the Bishop of London to notify him of her intention to attend his service the next day and claim sanctuary. On 10 July 1914, Norah went to Westminster Abbey and interrupted the Bishop of London, who was preaching at the 3.00 pm service, by stepping out and seeking sanctuary, shouting 'My Lord. In the name of God, stop forcible feeding. I myself am a prisoner under the Cat and Mouse Act, and will be arrested on leaving the Abbey'. At this point she was led out of the Abbey, rearrested and taken back to Holloway.[99] Presumably she or the Bishop had notified the authorities of her intention to go to Westminster Abbey and cause a disturbance, and, therefore, achieve her aim to be rearrested to generate publicity. Norah's target as ever was a Protestant leader, and she was taken immediately to Holloway where she began another hunger and thirst strike and was subjected to forcible feeding.

Five days later on 15 July Norah was released from prison again. Norah returned to Knightsbridge Hall with dramatic emphasis, echoing Annie Kenney's appearance on a stretcher at an earlier meeting:

Mrs Dacre Fox Appears – Warm Reception

Before the audience had time to recover, another surprise was awaiting them. A figure in white was seen to come to the front of the platform, and great enthusiasm was manifested when Mrs Dacre Fox was recognised. She looked very pale, and only spoke for a few minutes, but her words were so full of fire and enthusiasm that the audience listened spell bound. She then put the resolution, which was carried unanimously.[100]

In her speech, she defies her licence and determined not to let go of the Ulster parallel, she adopts their slogan, 'No Surrender':

'Stone walls do not a prison make, nor iron bars a cage,' and so it is has been possible – because those hackneyed and familiar words are as true today as when they were written – it has been possible for us who have broken down prison walls, and torn down iron bars, to send once more the message of this Union to the contemptible Government, and to the whole world. It is: 'No surrender: even unto death'.[101]

Norah's last arrest under her Cat and Mouse licence was on 30 July 1914 when she was arrested at Buckingham Palace delivering a letter from Mrs Pankhurst to the King.[102] After demanding to see the King's Secretary, plain clothes detectives arrested her as soon as she was recognised and took her to Holloway. Meanwhile a young suffragette had chained herself to the Buckingham Palace railings, and was explaining to all why Mrs Dacre Fox had wished to deliver a letter to the king. The young girl valiantly complained that Sir Edward Carson, who had encouraged and incited murder, was able to be received at the palace, while a women who was found guilty only of destroying property, was taken away to face a further hunger and thirst strike and force feeding for her conviction.[61] The exact date of Norah's release following this third imprisonment is not known. It seems these latter stages of Norah's prison career are less well documented in the media, perhaps because the imminence of war began to take up the interests of the nation and the nation's press.

Britain declared war on Germany on 4 August 1914. The government declared on 10 August that all remaining suffragette prisoners would be released and Mrs Pankhurst suspended militancy, requesting all WSPU members to devote their efforts to supporting the war. However, on 27 August, 14 suffragettes including Norah, Flora Drummond and Mary Richardson wrote letters addressed to Home Secretary McKenna, asking him to see them to discuss forcible feeding.[103]

According to Cowman[104] all 14 women went in a deputation to the Home Office to hand in letters and press their case about ongoing forcible feeding despite the declared government amnesty. The reasons were two fold. Irish suffragettes were excluded from the amnesty and were still subject to forcible feeding. Secondly, despite the government amnesty for the remaining suffragette prisoners, the situation regarding the 'mice' (a popular term coined at the time to describe women out of prison on licence under the Cat and Mouse legislation) was unclear as their sentences had not been formally ended by the authorities. As a result some women who had started going about their normal business were being rearrested, taken back to prison and being force fed. It appears that the authorities then announced that to resolve this problem, women who were still on licence should present themselves at the last prison they had been held in, where the necessary paperwork would be dealt with and their sentences formally ended.

As a result of this demonstration Norah was rearrested and taken back to Holloway. However, there is no record of her being held or force fed again, and it is assumed that the authorities did as outlined above, and formally completed the paperwork to end Norah's sentence, along with any of the other 14 women in the same position.

Norah Dacre Fox circa 1913 © Museum of London

Suffragette Medal, Norah Dacre Fox

Photograph courtesy of Spink and Son Ltd

Suffragette Medal, Norah Dacre Fox

Photograph courtesy of Spink and Son Ltd

Hand written letter: 'To the Home Secretary, Dear Sir, As a prisoner temporarily released under the Cat and Mouse Act, I am desirous of seeing you with reference to the alleged amnesty of suffragist prisoners. Yours faithfully, Norah Dacre Fox. 27 August 1914'.

Original held at the National Archives, London

CALLING ALL WOMEN

PATRIOT GAMES

The outbreak of war in 1914 caused some disorientation amongst the suffragette leadership. Both Emmeline and Christabel Pankhurst initially took the stance that the war was the natural outcome of the male predisposition to dominate and keep women in subjection stating that 'War is not women's way! To the women of this union human life is sacred!'.[105] However, the Pankhursts soon realised that this view would sideline the WSPU and in the words of Jessie Stephen (a former WSPU member) Emmeline, Christabel and their coterie turned 'all patriotic' and fully espoused the war.[106]

Sylvia Panhkhurst, a committed socialist, split with her mother and sister around this time, objecting to their right wing patriotic drift. Sylvia formed the East London Federation of Suffragettes (ELF), a breakaway group of the WSPU. Jessie Stephen was one of Sylvia's followers. Stephen was born in Scotland, and was brought up in a firmly socialist household, with strong allegiance to the Labour Party. As a socialist and pacifist, she found herself most closely aligned with Sylvia's ELF. When interviewed in 1977, Stephen[106] described the WSPU as consisting broadly of two parts, the 'working women' who had done most of the difficult front line militant work, and the upper class women, who dominated the leadership roles. Stephen, like Sylvia, opposed the strongly patriotic stance of the WSPU that was emerging in the build up to war. In her interview, Stephen referred to 'All that crowd ….. Dacre Fox and the Pankhursts ….', implying that Norah was a member of a close cadre of middle and upper class conservative women leading the WSPU. 'Mrs Dacre Fox became prominent toward the end – professional woman, middle class – I don't know what she was actually in her profession – because she was a very good speaker – a fine speaker – and very effective too'.

This volte-face by Emmeline Pankhurst, supported by Christabel, when she declared her truce in August 1914 and suspended militancy, was total and complete. All their subsequent actions were as extreme in their attempts to demonstrate their patriotism, support for the Government, anti-pacifist and anti-German views as they had been in their extreme demonstration of disdain for the actions of the Government in opposing votes for women up to that point. Grace Roe[48] defended the Pankhursts' pro-war position on the grounds that if Germany were to win the war under the Kaiser, who represented Prussian authoritarianism, women's suffrage and their struggle for rights would be completely set back. Other commentators suggest that the Pankhursts' move was primarily to save the WSPU from extinction and loss of influence.

Emmeline Pankhurst quickly got to work justifying why the WSPU had abandoned the suffrage struggle to support the war effort. Grace Roe, Norah's great friend and confidante, organised the campaign for Mrs Pankhurst, which was launched on 21 September 1914[107] when she spoke at the Brighton Dome. In her speech Mrs Pankhurst publicly abandoned pacifist beliefs and embraced the 'righteousness' of the war. Norah also spoke, calling on 'The young men of the nation to answer Lord Kitchener's call for fresh reinforcements'.[108] In November 1914 Norah worked with Lady Nancy Astor arranging for Mrs Pankhurst to give a speech in Plymouth, the Astors' constituency where Nancy enjoyed as much popular political appeal as her husband who was the MP for the area.[109]

Mrs Pankhurst's new ideology saw her espouse national unity and vociferously promote the call for women to become actively involved in war work by taking on jobs that had traditionally been regarded as in the male preserve, given that those men were now absent at the front. This was set in train through the pages of The Suffragette, relaunched on 16 April 1915 with the slogan that it was 'a thousand times more the duty of the militant Suffragettes to fight the Kaiser for the sake of liberty than it was to fight anti-Suffrage Governments'.[107]

During June 1915 the King had enquired of Government ministers whether they would be able to persuade women to enlist in war work to overcome the shortage of male workers by making use of Mrs Pankhurst. This gave Mrs Pankhurst the platform to launch a campaign to recruit women to work in factories, again organised for her by Grace Roe. Roe was given money from the Ministry of Munition's propaganda fund to organise a march from the Thames Embankment to the Ministry offices in London demanding the right for women to be employed in war work.[110]

During 1915 the Government became faced with a labour shortage aggravated by industrial unrest, while simultaneously needing to enlist more volunteers for the front line in France. Labour unrest reached a crescendo when strikes broke out in the South Wales coalfields in July 1915 in support of a 20% pay rise, but more generally countrywide trade union opposition to war work exacerbated their difficulties. For Emmeline Pankhurst these difficulties provided the perfect platform to further her crusade to give women the right to be employed in war work and munitions factories, while at the same time campaigning for the war effort, encouraging men to enlist, and arguing against trade union opposition. Trade union opposition to the war effort was regarded by her as evidence of socialist and Bolshevik influences misleading workers into strikes in areas like South Wales which were seen as 'red'.

The WSPU's rightward swing in response to this labour unrest was evidenced during the autumn of 1915 when Norah accompanied Emmeline Pankhurst, Flora Drummond, Annie Kenney, Grace Roe and others to South Wales, the Midlands and Clydeside on a 'recruiting' and lecture tour to encourage trade unions to support war work.[110] [107]

During the South Wales part of the tour on 27 September 1915[111] Mrs Pankhurst visited Glamorgan Colliery at Tonypandy with Norah, Miss Wickham and Miss Johnson in tow. They had an underground tour, visiting seams and observing coal cutting. On the surface they were taken to a laboratory and given a taste of German gas, which apparently 'affected Mrs Dacre Fox'. Mrs Pankhurst's report of this visit to the Guardian reporter reads like part of a right wing government propaganda campaign with references to 'improved conditions under which the colliers now work' and how the strike had arisen 'due to the fact that people do not realise the fact that war is going on'. Mrs Pankhurst further went on to suggest that the government 'should arrange for parties of workmen and their wives to visit the theatre of war, and especially the scene of the recent Zeppelin raids'. It is hard to imagine how she could practically foresee this being organised.

On 15 October 1915 The Suffragette announced that it was changing its name to Britannia. Articles in this publication now concentrated heavily on campaigning and lobbying on the war and organising meetings and events, which were usually advertised as 'A Patriotic Meeting'. They focused on criticizing Germany and all Germans who were living and working in England, particularly in the higher echelons of the civil service. This particular campaign was to occupy Norah intensely and engage her in a new cause that would eventually take her away from the Pankhurst cadre to continue campaigning after the end of the war.

The immediate cause of WW1 had been a declaration of war by Austria-Hungary on Serbia after Serbian assassins had killed Archduke Franz Ferdinand and his wife in June 1914. The complicated alliances of the Balkan countries at this historical juncture saw Turkey and its Bulgarian ally line up with Austria-Hungary against Serbia and its Greek allies. The Suffragette and Britannia consistently portray Serbia as a victim, a theme also taken up by Emmeline Pankhurst during her seven month lecture tour of America from January 1916, undertaken partly to raise money for Serbia. Articles in Britannia show an ongoing concern that Serbia was at risk of being betrayed by the British. There were concerns for example that a Foreign Office official with connections to German Naval War Staff could or might influence the 'betrayal' of Serbia.[112] Britannia took up and echoed a vigorous concern among the tabloid right-wing press, specifically the Daily Mail edited by Lord Northcliffe,[113] that the Balkan policy of the Foreign Minister, Sir Edward Grey, was inadequate, was prolonging the war, had failed to protect Serbia and was failing to honour its allegiances to Greece and Rumania.[114]

Although Norah and the Pankhursts were now entering mainstream politics rather than their former anti-establishment politics, they did not adapt their style of language accordingly, and were often openly hostile and inflammatory towards their targets. In aligning themselves with Lord Northcliffe's Daily Mail, they placed themselves somewhat on the right-wing fringe in the campaign against Sir Edward Grey and continued to resort to violence to make themselves heard.[115] Mrs

Pankhurst had called an end to suffragette violence, but reports in Britannia of women being arrested for violent anti-government demonstrations on war issues appears to suggest that she either condoned the continued use of violence or, alternatively, was having difficulty in restraining the militancy that had been unleashed during the suffragette campaign. The 'Liberal Press' which included The Times condemned the Daily Mail's attacks on Sir Edward Grey and accused the 'minority' press for scapegoating him instead of supporting the Government at a time of need.[116]

The WSPU held numerous open air and indoor meetings on the war situation at various venues, including the Albert Hall and Hyde Park. Norah spoke on at least 13 reported occasions, two of these at the end of processions to Trafalgar Square where speakers would address the crowd standing between Landseer's two stone lions at the base of Nelson's column. Public speaking on this scale was inevitably challenging and impressive, requiring a very loud and well projected voice given that there were no loudspeakers to assist the speaker in being heard by the throngs of people filling the square. Surviving Pathé newsreel[117] shows Norah accompanied by Mrs Pankhurst at Trafalgar Square going up to speak on the 'Rumanian Crisis' in November 1916.

> *Let me now turn to the point of view of our own national salvation. In leaving Greece in the state in which she is today, we have created in the Balkans a situation from which it will take us a long and uncertain time to recover. It has been said that Rumania entered into war on the understanding that there*

would be a strong offensive in Macedonia with the Salonica forces. General Sarrail cannot do this while Greece is in the state she is today.

I urge the people here to rouse public opinion and support M Venizelos in the magnificent fight that he is making in the cause of the Allies and the cause of freedom.[118]

The propensity of Norah and her colleagues for personalising some of their campaign speeches and directly criticising politicians by name led to one meeting advertised for the Kingsway Hall being cancelled by the Trustees on the grounds that they could not allow criticism of individual members of the Government. The WSPU was, therefore, forced to make alternative arrangements and hold the meetings at the WSPU HQ in Portland Place over three days 12-14 April 1916. Norah chaired all three meetings and spoke at each one.[119]

The language used in Norah's speeches continued to be forceful and her speeches appeared in Britannia under headings such as 'Grey had betrayed Rumania as he betrayed Serbia', 'What about the crippling of the British Navy', 'Traitor Grey!' Norah would often speak of the 'necessity of increased efforts in England to combat German intrigue'. On 9 November 1916[120] Norah was reported in The Guardian as accompanying Mrs Pankhurst to the Houses of Parliament to see Viscount Grey to present him with a 'resolution about King Constantine'. The article suggests that this happened on more than one occasion, with Mrs Pankhurst regularly being refused admittance. On this occasion she adopted the old suffragette tactic of stating that she would remain 'by the doorway until the House rose' in which action she was supported by Mrs Dacre Fox; it seems some kind person also provided her 'with a stool' to aid her during her wait. This was a well rehearsed tactic having been used by Norah in previous direct action campaigns as already noted. Norah's final speech in this particular campaign was on 20 November 1916[121] at a mass meeting in 'Honour of the Allied Nations' held at the Queen's Hall.

During 1916 and 1917, in addition to taking part in this vigorous patriotic campaign, Norah was working in part time paid employment on a government commission concerning the work of the Medical Research Council, supervising a typing pool. This work may have been necessary to support her financially at this time, but it also helped her gather information required for a campaign she would wage some years later against the medical establishment (see The Good Body).

ENEMY ALIEN PERIL

In November 1917, Britannia[122] announced on its front page 'the WSPU will henceforward be known as The Women's Party'. This marked yet another milestone in the public activities of Emmeline and Christabel Pankhurst, and the coterie that supported them, including

Annie Kenney, Flora Drummond and Grace Roe. Norah did not join the Women's Party and began to develop her political career independently of her former colleagues. Despite confusion amongst commentators on links with various women's organisations during this period, Norah's campaigning after 1917 was all undertaken independently. This was made clear by a notice she had published in the Times which read 'It was stated in The Times last Saturday that Mrs Dacre Fox was connected with the Women's Freedom League. We are asked by Mrs Fox to state that she is not connected with any League'.[123]

Norah's new campaign drew on the rising tide of anti-German sentiment in England. Anti-German feeling rose particularly high as a result of Germany's policy of Unrestricted Submarine Warfare (USW). The policy caused worldwide outrage and condemnation, particularly after a German submarine sank the Lusitania, a passenger ship, on 7 May 1915 killing 1198 civilians, 128 of whom were Americans. The incident caused widespread rioting and anger and excited extremely hostile press articles. As a result of this worldwide outrage Germany suspended USW, but reinstated this policy later in the war, a factor which directly contributed to the extreme level of hostility against aliens in Britain during and after WW1. The USW policy was deliberately adopted by Germany in order to restrict the amount of goods and materials getting to Britain, and led directly to rationing and shortages in Britain towards the end of the war and its immediate aftermath. One result of the intensity of anti-German feeling in Britain was that the British royal family changed its name from Saxe-Coburg-Gotha to Windsor.

Reflecting the anti-German sentiment, the British Empire Union was created in 1916 after changing its name from the Anti-German Union founded in 1915. This organisation was responsible for many of the London demonstrations during this period, whipping up public feeling about the enemy alien threat. Another anti-German organisation was the National Party, created in 1917 as a right wing split from the Conservative Party. Its leaders were Lord Ampthill, Sir Richard Cooper and Sir Henry Page Croft MP, and its main plank was its intensely xenophobic reaction to WW1, although before the 1918 election most of its members had defected to rejoin the Conservatives.

Norah does not appear to have been a member of either organisation, but both the National Party and the British Empire Union led, or were involved in, the demonstrations that gave Norah a high public profile during her anti-alien campaign, with many of their prominent leaders sharing platforms with her during this period. The first major rally Norah organised took place on 13 July 1918 in Trafalgar Square,[124] Norah had advertised the rally in the Times[125] and had spent much time and preparation canvassing prominent figures for their backing, many of whom sent letters of support which she read out at the rally including The Lord Mayor of London, The Bishop of Birmingham, Rudyard Kipling, Harry Lauder and Mr Massey the Prime Minister of New Zealand. Speakers at the rally included the Mayors of

Bury St Edmonds, Canterbury and Stoke Newington, as well as Sir Alexander Bannerman and Major General Sir Hugh MacCalmont.

The Mayor of London had in fact agreed to chair the rally, but according to the Times 'In the unavoidable absence of the Mayor, who had hoped to preside, the chair was taken by Mr J Doherty',[124] It seems Norah had persuaded her father to step in at the last minute, indicating that they were on good enough terms at this point to work together on a shared political concern. Later in 1918 John Doherty also arranged the printing of campaign posters on his own printing press indicating that whether or not he was supporting Norah financially at this time, he was prepared to give material support to her work,[126] Evidence supporting this also appears in a speech reported in a press cutting (unable to identify paper or date) attributed to John Doherty at a Liberal Club dinner hosted in his honour by members of the Spelthorne Magistrate's Bench. He was referred to as having a 'strong and patriotic attitude concerning Germans, naturalised and unnaturalised' to which John Doherty is reported to have made 'an eloquent reply in which he denounced a flabby attitude towards pacifists and Germans masquerading in naturalisation dress'.

Norah's rallying speech in Trafalgar Square was vigorous as ever, but she determined to make it clear that she would not be turning to militant methods as she had done in the past: The Times report of the rally records that - 'She had received suggestions from various quarters that if immediate action was not taken by the

Government the people should take the matter into their own hands. She would be no party to anything of the kind. Until everything was done that could be done in a constitutional manner violence would be outrageous'.[124]

After this first rally, a series of letters were exchanged between Norah and the Prime Minister Lloyd George, printed in full in the Times. Norah requested that the Prime Minister receive a deputation. This was refused on the grounds that Parliament had dealt with the matter. Norah responded that the measures announced in the Houses of Parliament 'were not in any sense sufficiently drastic to satisfy the national demand, and that the resolution I enclosed in my letter to you of the 15th described those proposals as 'futile and useless to deal with the alien enemy danger'.[127]

Other meetings and rallies throughout the country organised by the National Party or the British Empire Union were regularly reported on in the Times. All called for resolutions along the same extreme lines, demanding for example, that 'the government shall immediately intern and deport when the war is over all persons of enemy origin; further that no person of enemy origin shall enter any part of the Empire for at least 10 years after the war...'.[128] The demand for deportation included all those of German origin whether naturalised or not. Many of the meetings were held by workers associations such as the Liverpool Cotton Association, the Cardiff Sailors' and Firemen's Union, demanding the dismissal and deportation of enemy workers in their midst.

Over the next seven months Norah delivered regular speeches all over London including 21 July 1918 at Hyde Park,[128] 25 July 1918 to members of the Baltic Exchange at Merchant's Hall,[129] 30 July 1918 at the Royal Albert Hall,[130] 16 August 1918 at Cannon Street Hotel[131] and 28 August 1918 at a Master Bakers' Meeting, Camberwell.[132] There were several large demonstrations in Hyde Park and Trafalgar Square, favourite locations of the WSPU, and which Norah would have been very experienced in organising. Norah also wrote to all Mayors countrywide, asking them to hold public meetings to consider the 'alien question' and to form local committees of public safety composed of men and women.[133] The purpose of these local committees was to organise campaigns to put pressure on local MPs and threaten them with deselection if they did not support the anti-alien campaign.

Norah's rhetoric throughout this campaign was extreme in its demands, yet it stopped short of inciting public violence against aliens and insisted that any violence should be legally administered:

> *Mrs Dacre Fox said that for the first time since the war broke out there was an open fight between the British public and German influence at work in this country. We had to make a clean sweep of all persons of German blood, without distinction of sex, birthplace, or nationality. Never had the time been so ripe for action; never would it be so favourable again. If we allowed the opportunity to pass now, German influence, which at the present moment was hampering and hindering the War Cabinet in its prosecution of the war, would become more firmly entrenched than ever in this country. The report of the*

Committee set up by Mr Lloyd George was an exceedingly weak report, and its recommendations were useless. They wanted to see every person of German blood in this country under lock and key. They must make the politicians move. Any person in this country, no matter who he was or what his position, who was suspected of protecting German influence, should be tried as a traitor, and, if necessary, shot. There must be no compromise and no discrimination.

If British people were shut up – not interned – in Germany during the war, where would their sympathies and hearts be? Why here, of course, and anybody who said the contrary was talking nonsense. If the Germans here were not loyal to their own country, how could they be loyal to ours? They did not want German loyalty. (Cheers). It was a sign of decadence to ask for it. They did not want the enemy to help us in any capacity whatever. To expect it was un-British, and contrary to the spirit and traditions which built up the Empire. The Home Office was impregnated with German influence, and the Foreign Office used men protected by the Home Office.[134]

The rallies and demonstrations grew in momentum, with more and more publicity and coverage in the national press. Some 8,000 people attended the Royal Albert Hall on 30 July 1918. Clearly the campaign organisers had been successful in gaining significant funding for the movement, since meetings were free to attend and venues such as the Royal Albert Hall could not be hired cheaply.

At the Hyde Park rally on 24 August 1918, the National Party revealed that their petition had received 1,250,000 signatories, measured over two miles in length and was to be handed to the Prime Minister. Five platforms had been erected in Hyde Park each with huge banners above them.[135] General Page Croft MP is described as 'taking the first platform, and the other speakers were Mr Leo Maxse and Mrs Dacre Fox'. The other four platforms each had a chairman and speakers, among them trade union leaders and Mr JG Jenkins, late premier of South Australia. The supporters of the British Empire Union gathered at platform three.

> *Mrs Dacre Fox said that she was convinced that the efforts of the fighting forces on land and sea, and the sacrifices of civilians at home, were being largely nullified by enemy aliens being allowed to remain at large in our midst. Our whole life, political, social and financial, was permeated by German influence, which was aiming at reducing the condition of this country to the condition of Russia. She had in her possession official documents, which the Government also held, proving that men had been appointed on the boards of great shipping firms in order to gain information of the sailing vessels, and that when vessels had sailed they were torpedoed.*

The petition was then taken to Downing Street:

> *It..... was carried from Hyde Park to Downing Street in a lorry decorated with the Union Jack, the Stars and Stripes, the French Tricolour and the flags of other allied nations, accompanied by a procession with bands and banners almost as long as itself. The procession was headed by an immense white*

sheet from which stood out prominently the inscription:– 'The National Party, backed by the nation, demands the internment of all enemy aliens'. In the marching ranks were members of the Provisional Grand Council of the National Party, thousands of discharged soldiers and sailors, branches of the British Empire Union, deputations from Committees of Public Safety formed in various cities and towns of the country, Dominion soldiers, trade unions, and a great array of the general public, men and women, which included many representative City men of the Baltic and the Stock Exchange. The route lay through Oxford-Street, Regent-Street, and Cockspur-Street to Trafalgar Square, where the procession waited until the return of the deputation from Downing Street.[135]

While in certain respects Norah's rhetoric was extreme, she did suggest that action taken against aliens should be legal. This same courtesy, however, was not extended to British politicians despite her earlier insistence at her Trafalgar Square rally on 13 July 1918 that militancy should not be used except as a last resort. Clearly by 2 September 1918[136] she had personally run out of patience as the Guardian reported on a meeting held on Plumstead Common (near Woolwich, London) the previous Saturday. The meeting had been arranged by the Independent Labour Party and Ramsay MacDonald MP was to address the meeting. A counter demonstration was organised by the Royal Arsenal Branch of the National Federation of Discharged and Demobilised Sailors and Soldiers. This group arrived on the Common carrying banners with slogans such as "All patriots; so to hell with Ramsay MacDonald and his German comrades." A Mr Roderick led this demonstration, declaring that when Mr MacDonald rose to speak Mrs Dacre Fox and Mr Stubbs would 'mount the platform and ask him three questions; "Are you out to win the war?" "Are you a friend or enemy of Germany?" "Are you wishing for a peace at Germany's price?" Their declared tactic, in the event they did not get satisfactory answers was that 'the platform would be stormed and they would all take part in the fight'. It appears that this was the eventual outcome as the article reports that the meeting did indeed degenerate into 'Free fights, stone-throwing, combats with sticks and riotous proceedings'.

It was during this period from July until November 1918 that the English became increasingly convinced of victory in the war, and part of this anti-German feeling and jingoistic rhetoric was aimed at pre-empting an armistice and end to the war. The enemy alien campaign was clearly not just about removing Germans from England, but was about how to punish the German nation once they had been defeated. At the Albert Hall on 2 November 1918, as armistice was drawing near, Norah and her co-campaigners spoke about the peace negotiations and demanded of them to 'let the enemy know he could expect no mercy' and that the preconditions for any negotiations were that the Kaiser and his Government offered unconditional surrender. The matter of indemnities that Germany had been asking for were dismissed by the platform speakers, who insisted that Germany should be paying the indemnities, not the Allies.[137]

A Clean Sweep Poster, 1918

An original is held at The Imperial War Museum

QUALIFICATION OF WOMEN ACT

On 19 June 1917 the House of Commons had passed Clause IV of the Representation of the People Bill entitling women aged 30 and over with household qualifications to vote. Parliamentary opinion had dramatically shifted, and the Bill was passed with a majority of 285 to 55. Welcome as this was, however, it was a further ten years until the Fifth Reform Bill was passed in 1928 and women were given the right to vote on the same basis as men. Nevertheless, Emmeline, Christabel and their coterie, which could be called the rump of the WSPU by this time, made much of this partial victory.

On 16 March 1918 the former WSPU held a large meeting at the Royal Albert Hall, advertised as The Women's Victory – Celebration of Suffrage Victory. All Suffragettes who endured force feeding were presented with medals by Mrs Pankhurst. Norah was awarded a medal with three bars representing the three times she had been imprisoned.[138] Norah it seems was evidently still on good terms with the Pankhursts even if she was now forging her own political path.

WWI ended famously at 11am on 11 November 1918 and a General Election was held in December. Women already had the right to vote, but the Parliament

(Qualification of Women) Act 1918 was required to grant the 'Capacity of Women to sit in Parliament' enabling them to stand as parliamentary candidates. Many of Norah's former WSPU colleagues stood for election within the main political parties. Although the National Party with whom Norah was closely affiliated, put forward candidates for election, Norah did not stand for them, and instead entered the hustings as an Independent for Richmond. Norah stood against Walter Crotch (Independent), Clifford Edgar (Coalition Unionist) and RJ Morrison (Liberal) none of whom had been a Member of Parliament previously.[139]

Norah's election campaign was a straightforward continuation of her enemy alien campaign, and as such would have been very similar to those candidates standing for the National Party. This raises the question, therefore, as to whether she chose not to join the party, or whether they chose not to put her forward as a candidate, thereby forcing her to stand as an Independent. The National Party did not, however, put up a candidate against her. We must assume that without party support, Norah was self-funding, perhaps with the support of her father. By this time she had given up her paid work at the MRC, and as far as is known was not in any new employment. Norah lost the election winning just 3,615 votes; the seat being won by Edgar the Coalition candidate. In all 16 women stood for parliament, but the only woman to get elected was Constance Markievicz, who won a seat as a Sinn Fein candidate for South Dublin. Markievicz, however, did not take her seat as it was Sinn Fein's policy not to recognise the English parliament's rule over Ireland; in any case Markievicz was serving a prison sentence for her part in the Dublin uprising in 1916.

The anti-alien 'agitation' carried on after 1918, widening into a campaign against not just 'enemy' aliens but also 'friendly' aliens who had become British subjects through naturalisation.[140] Remaining involved with this movement, Norah tried to begin a series of initiatives, which did not, it seems, come to fruition. These included a meeting on the 'Defence of British Rights in Britain' in February 1919[141] and the organisation of a National Safety Movement 'with the object of fighting the German garrison in Great Britain... to make it unlawful for any person of German birth, including German-Austrians, to enter, land or reside in any part of the British Isles'. The aim was to secure the drafting of legislation ensuring naturalisation rules were changed to prevent Germans voting in Parliamentary or Municipal elections, or holding Government or civil service positions.[142] Along with the British Empire Union, Norah also gave support in March 1919 to the Variety Artists' Federation who were protesting about German performers being allowed to take up employment in Britain while British artists, demobbed soldiers in particular, could not get work.[143]

Although virulently xenophobic and to modern minds vicious, Norah's enemy alien campaign, ironically, had largely remained on the right side of the law, unlike her previous suffrage campaigns, where the underlying democratic principles were, to modern minds, wholly justified. Nevertheless, Norah did find herself subject to yet another libel action as a result of her anti-German tirade. Sir Alfred Mond, 1st Baron Melchett PC, FRS was a third generation German immigrant naturalised in the 1880s. His father was acclaimed as the father of British industrial chemistry and had businesses in Britain and Canada, without the support of which it was claimed, Britain 'could not have won the war'. Sir Alfred was a significant figure in British public life in both business and politics. Political appointments during a parliamentary career saw him serving in the coalition government of David Lloyd George as First Commissioner of Works from 1916 to 1921 and as Minister of Health (with a seat in cabinet) from 1921 to 1922. In business in 1926 he was to be pivotal in creating a merger of the four companies that became known as Imperial Chemical Industries (ICI), of which he became the first chairman.

During the 1918 election Sir Alfred stood for election for the seat of Swansea West, but was subjected to extreme xenophobia, later taking out libel actions against those he held responsible. Sir Alfred sued Norah and a colleague Mr Brook for making libellous speeches accusing him and his brother, Robert, of being German sympathisers, who had 'tried to supply Germany through Norway and Sweden during the war'. Sir Alfred also sued the editor of the South Wales Daily Post, Mr Davies, who had published extracts of these speeches.[144] Sir Alfred noted when giving evidence that 'what made the case more pitiable and more wretched' was that his only son had been severely wounded in the war while serving in the same British regiment as Mr Davies' son. Mr Davies apologised and the jury awarded Sir Alfred £500 damages. In a further libel case against a Mr Fraser, Sir Alfred was awarded £5,000. In both cases, the barrister for Sir Alfred was none other than Norah's old adversary, Sir Edward Carson.

Norah's anti-German campaign seemed to draw to a close some time during 1920 when her personal life was beginning to take a major turn. Provoked by concern over the Treaty of Versailles not being properly implemented by Germany, the last record of Norah's public campaigning was a letter in the Times on 10 April 1920:

> *No language can be too severe, and no protest too strong, against what amounts to a virtual betrayal of our Ally France. The question does not allow of argument. France is our friend. Upon her security and her prestige depend the security and prestige of the British Empire. One had imagined that this lesson had been fully learnt as the experience of the European War, and a policy which tends to weaken France must be a policy which helps to strengthen her enemy and ours – Germany. The truth is that in this country there are a group of politicians and public men, surrounded by officials and advisers, who have always worked and are still working for a rapprochement with Germany with the hope of a future alliance with her. This means that the Entente Cordiale must disappear, and that France will be left alone and Germany become the dominant Power on the Continent.*
>
> *What the people of this country want to know, once and for all, is whether this policy is the official policy of his Majesty's*

Government. If it be so, then British men and women have a right to be informed of such a momentous change in the foreign policy of this country. If it be not so, then they have an even stronger right to demand that Mr Lloyd George and his responsible colleagues shall carry out in the letter and the spirit the policy of friendship towards France. I have no hesitation in saying that the bulk of British public opinion is anti-German and pro-French in its widest sense, and that there is an overwhelming desire in this country to see that friendship cemented, strengthened, and supported under all circumstances.

That the British Government has first hesitated to stand by France in her legitimate action in insisting on the terms of the Treaty of Versailles being carried out by Germany, and then openly ranged itself against our Ally France, and on the side of our late enemy, Germany, is a proceeding of profound moment, and I ask space in your columns to urge the public to take every means which they possess without one moment's delay to convey to Mr Lloyd George their detestation of this treacherous action.[145]

Latterly, historians have generally agreed that the Treaty of Versailles and the harsh reparations foisted on to Germany as a result contributed, together with the financial crisis of the 1920s embodied in the Wall Street Crash, to fuel the terrible poverty and massive inflation that endured in Germany during the 1920s and 1930s. However, the rise of Hitler and the Second World War were a long way off at this point, and it is obvious that Norah, and presumably a large part of the public, were still at this point nursing a xenophobic and unforgiving hangover of Germany from WW1.

The Wrong Side of the Bed

Although the seeds of a future extremist right wing agenda were sown, Norah's life seems to have changed significantly in the early 1920s, distracting her from vigorous campaign work. It transpired that Norah was not infertile after all and when in 1921 she went to see the doctor complaining of feeling unwell, he informed her that she was pregnant. Norah told the doctor that he was a fool and demanded a second opinion since she was not capable of having children.[31] However, on 29 May 1922 she gave birth to an illegitimate child. Although it is not known exactly when she moved out of London, by 1928 she was calling herself Norah Elam, had separated from Charles Dacre Fox, although still used the name Dacre Fox on occasions, and was living with Dudley Elam in Northchapel, West Sussex. Her son was known as Tony Elam, although his birth certificate records his name as Evelyn Anthony Christopher Fox.

To have an illegitimate child at this time would have been an outrage. Emmeline Pankhurst had felt so concerned about the moral depravity of infants born out of wedlock that she began a campaign through the WSPU in 1915 to encourage women in the WSPU to adopt illegitimate children and save them from an otherwise doomed existence. The campaign was based on an article in the British Medical Journal written by Dr Dingwall Fordyce who argued that while illegitimate children were born of 'degenerate parents', the infants could be saved from their inherited moral degeneracy.

> *As regards the moral inheritance, let us remember that the presence of the baby focuses attention on one particular sin on the part of the mother; the magnitude of which sin in each particular case, we are incapable of judging. The mirror of virtue is badly cracked by the birth of an illegitimate baby, but in many other cases there are numerous little cracks which en masse are hardly, if at all, less important. Heredity is universally accepted as a most important moral and physical element in the life of man, as witness the modern 'science' of Eugenics. But heredity merges in environment. Be we as scientific as we may, we cannot define the border between the two and good nurture has for ages been efficacious in developing the best and controlling the lower innate potentialities. (Dr Fordyce, quoted in The Suffragette)[146]*

Mrs Pankhurst went on to open an adoption home in Campden Hill for war babies which was a progressive move for her time as she came under much criticism for giving sanctuary to illegitimate children. However, although Mrs Pankhurst was willing to face criticism for saving these depraved infants, her campaign left little doubt as to her view of their mothers. When Sylvia Pankhurst gave birth to an illegitimate child in 1927, her mother with whom relations were already strained, refused to see her ever again; Emmeline Pankhurst never met her grandchild.

Although Norah's political move away from the Pankhursts and her friend Grace Roe did not seem acrimonious at the time, she did eventually lose touch with her old friends. Norah's right wing leap could not have concerned them greatly as they largely espoused the same ideas. However, Norah's fall from grace in giving birth to an illegitimate child may well have begun the process of estrangement from her former colleagues and friends in the WSPU as well as the Dohertys. Emmeline Pankhurst died in 1928 and Christabel had moved to America in 1921. Grace Roe later became the President of The Suffragette Fellowship, producing a yearly newsletter 'Calling All Women'[147] between 1951 and 1977. As editor of the newsletter, Roe did not mention Norah once in it, not even in an obituary. In an interview in 1974, Roe commented that she had lost touch and had no idea whatsoever had happened to Norah,[48] but given Norah's ongoing presence in the political arena this seems unlikely to be true. Jessie Stephen, also interviewed in the 1970s remembered very clearly what had happened to Norah ('She got tied up with the Fascist movement') and Jessie was not anywhere near as close to Norah as Grace Roe had been; it therefore seems likely that Grace fell out with Norah at some point, perhaps because of the shameful path she took in living in sin and having an illegitimate child. Norah herself went to great lengths to cover up these shameful facts when she met her new political colleagues in the 1930s.

ROYAL ANCESTRY

Dudley, whose full name was Edward Descou Dudley Vallance Elam, was born in 1872, the son of Frederick William Elam and Carina Overall Marie Julie Descou Elam. The couple had been married in 1868, in the presence of Carina's father, Peter Descou, and her sister, Julie Descou.[148] The marriage certificate records Frederick and Carina's fathers as 'gentlemen' indicating that they were wealthy and of private means. Frederick William Elam was in fact the son of Thomas William Elam and Ann Vallance who had married in Hove in 1822.[149] The Vallance family were a long established wealthy land owning family from the Brighton and Hove area, and Dudley's first cousin once removed was John Olliver Vallance, responsible for building Brooker Hall in Hove in 1877, named for his father John Brooker Vallance, Anne's brother. Brooker Hall now houses the Hove Museum and Art Gallery.

It seems that there was a tradition in the Vallance and Elam family to claim historically important kinship ties. The Vallance family claim was to have descended from Aymer de Valence, 2nd Earl of Pembroke, whose father was a half brother of Henry III. Dudley clearly decided to carry on this Vallance family ritual bestowing on both children from his first marriage Carina and Eustace, a middle name of De Valence.[150] However, it was his mother Carina's ancestry that was to assume a huge importance in Norah's self-presentation, although she was clearly spoiled for choice in deciding which claim to famous ancestors would enhance her public profile most.

Carina's parents, Peter (born in England in 1811) and Julie Josephine Neeteson (born in Ghent in 1818)[151] had met and married in Ghent, once part of the French Empire and now part of Belgium. Peter Descou came from the well-to-do Descou (or Decew) family that had immigrated to England from Valenciennes in France in the 17th century. Other branches of the family immigrated to Canada founding Decewville and naming the Decew Falls.[152] Peter had left England to work in Ghent as a toolmaker. Their first son, Arthur, was born in Ghent in 1840, followed by Carina in 1846 and Petrus in 1848.[153] By 1852 the family had moved to England where Peter Descou was appointed as a booking clerk at Tonbridge railway station. He was later promoted to station master at Wadhurst railway station, Sussex, and by 1867 had become station master at Hastings. At the time railways were a new development of the modern world and to be involved in railways was considered prestigious and exciting. In 1855 another daughter, Julie Marie was born.

Sadly, Petrus died in his father's arms of scarlet fever, diarrhoea and peritonitis at Wadhurst Station in 1856.[154] He was eight years old at the time. Arthur had married by 1861 and was working as a railway clerk in Ashford, Kent,[155] but he contracted tuberculosis the next year and died in 1864.[156] These two would-be uncles of Dudley both died young; yet his mother Carina and his aunt Julie

Marie survived. Recent research has revealed that Carina was at some point adopted by her childless aunt Carina Day who was a wealthy business woman running a dressmaker and millinery business in Bruton Street, Berkeley Square, London. Carina Day's will left over £30,000 (equivalent to £1.76 million in 2010) in Trusts to various friends, family and charities including £3,000 in Trust for her adopted daughter Carina Descou providing her and any children with a significant income for life.[157] Carina Day specified that no husband could have any access to this inheritance. The significance of the Descou family to Norah was that she believed Carina's real mother, Julie Josephine Neeteson, to be the illegitimate daughter of Oscar Bernadotte, King of Sweden and Norway.

Ensconced in Norah's bedroom at Gothic Cottage in the 1950s, her granddaughters would regularly be called in to attend an 'audience' with Norah. On the wall were two oil paintings, believed to be original. These portraits, according to Norah, were of the sisters Julie Marie Bonaparte née Clary and her sister Bernardine Eugénie Désirée Bernadotte née Clary.[31] Julie Clary married Napoleon Bonaparte's brother, Joseph, and became Queen Consort of Naples and Sicily. Désirée, who was at one time engaged to marry Napoleon Bonaparte herself, eventually married General Jean-Baptiste Bernadotte, who became the adopted King of Sweden when the original Swedish Royal family died out. As a consequence Bernadine (known as Désirée) was crowned Queen of Sweden. According to Norah, Désirée and Bernadotte's only son, Oscar, who inherited his father's throne on his death, was Dudley's great grandfather.[31]

Oscar Bernadotte was known to have had illegitimate children, the first, 'Oscaria' being born in 1819 to Jaquette Lowenstein. No historical record is known to suggest that Oscar had another child the year before this. Julie Neeteson was indeed an illegitimate child ('fille naturelle') born to Marie Jeanne Neeteson, with no father's name recorded on her birth certificate.[151] One of the witnesses to the birth was the surgeon Francois Bernard Van Coppenole, who lived in the same street as the Neetesons. Throughout Van Coppenole's life and medical practice he built up a significant collection of medical, science and natural history literature, together with surgical instruments. This collection was considered so significant that a catalogue of his collection is held in the Cambridge University Library archive. His status and importance suggests that the Neetesons had some degree of social standing and wealth, but does not confirm that he was engaged by Oscar to assist in the birth of an illegitimate child.

In Julie's old age she lived with her daughter Carina, her son-in-law Frederick and her grandson Dudley Elam. Later in her old age she moved to live with Carina's younger sister Julie and husband Arthur Wiley until her death in 1902. Her death certificate records her name as Julie Josephine *Bernardine* Descou,[158] the Bernadine not having been present on her birth certificate, implying the adoption of the name by Julie during her life, perhaps because she believed she was connected to Désirée. Her mother may have told her this either because it was true or because she wanted her daughter to feel special in spite of being an illegitimate child, which carried severe social penalties.

However, while Oscar was known to have many lovers, Marie Jeanne Neeteson was never recorded as being one of them, and it seems unlikely to be true given that Oscar's known illegitimate children were not particularly well-kept secrets. Norah, however, remained absolutely convinced that Dudley's grandmother was the love child of King Oscar and would often talk about the novel Désirée by Annemarie Selinko,[159] angry that she had 'got it all wrong'.[31] Norah claimed that there were papers to prove the family genealogy held by 'Nanny Pannell' who was Tony's nanny. Why such papers would be given to a nanny employed by Norah and Dudley seems strange, and it is possible that Norah became somewhat confused in her later years, fixating on a need to justify her own fall from grace by emphasising the royal ancestry of her lover, and reminding herself that even royal families have illegitimate children. Dudley was nevertheless wealthy as he would have directly inherited the Trust given to his mother by Carina Day and he may well have also inherited money from his father Frederick Elam, giving him independent means.

Dudley's early education was by private tuition, following which he gained entry to Keeble College, Oxford University, graduating in 1893. He entered Oxford to study for a career as a clergyman in the Church of England, gaining a BA in 1895 and an MA in 1899.

While studying for his MA, he was working at the Parish Church of St Augustine, Hackney Wick between 1897 and 1899.[160]

Dudley's tutor clearly thought very little of his scholarship and his character, and made comments on his record such as 'Regular, not strong work'; 'Absolutely regular, very poor work'; 'Do not feel sure that he is equal to it'; 'Mentally worried and so not very attentive'; 'Better for him to read for Pass School'; 'Still very solitary I fear'; 'Lives his own life - which is however wider than before'; 'Rather a failure'.[160]

Dudley's subsequent career as a clergyman seems to have had little more success than his academic career, seeing him move from St Augustine's, Hackney Wick to work at the Parish Church of St Faith, Stoke Newington from 1899-1901, and afterwards at the Parish Church of St Augustine, Highgate 1901-1904.[161] after which his career with the church seems to have ended. He never progressed to any particular high rank in the church which would have merited him being recorded in Crockfords, the UK directory of Anglican clergy. After 1904, there is no record of Dudley having employment in the church or anywhere else; and later in his life he is described as being a civil servant working for the Ministry of Health,[162] although he did provide private tuition to students into his old age.

In 1897 Dudley married Ada Matilda Strong Baber, who was ten years his senior. The couple had two children Carina Mary Laura De Valence Elam in 1901, and Eustace Digby De Valence Elam in 1905.[163] These two children were Tony Elam's half-siblings and yet Tony's family knew nothing about them prior to the genealogical research carried out for the purposes of this book.

Norah gave birth to her only son Evelyn Anthony Christopher Fox on 29 May 1922,[164] at which time Norah and the baby were living at 17 Scarsdale Terrace, London. The pregnancy came as a great shock to Norah who was 43 years old by this time. Everyone who knew her was never in any doubt that a baby was extremely unwelcome in her life, particularly Tony himself. Although known as Tony Elam, he knew full well that he was a 'bastard' and suffered deeply from the shame of this; indeed he often denied even knowing that his real surname was Fox and when he emigrated to South Africa in the 1960s he claimed he could not obtain a birth certificate to apply for a passport because the Public Records Office had no record of the birth of a Tony Elam on the given date. Although he must have known that his birth would have been registered under Norah's real name, he persisted in the illusion that his name was Tony Elam and swore an affidavit to that effect in order to be granted a passport to travel. Tony was so distraught about his bastardy that he had gone to any means necessary to get a passport showing his assumed surname of Elam.

On Tony's actual birth certificate Norah recorded her name as Norah Dacre Fox, formerly Doherty. Under the name of the father is the name 'George' crossed out. As remains the law today, if a mother wishes to register the name of the father on a birth certificate, he must be present if he is not the woman's husband. Although we assume that Dudley Elam was the child's father given that he assumed this role, Norah was clearly alone when she went to register the birth, and Norah in her own contrary way decided to give a name for the father which was neither Dudley nor Charles. We do not know what surname she gave, but whatever it was, the Registrar would have realised that it was not Dacre Fox, therefore not her husband and, therefore, could not be written on the certificate; hence he crossed out the 'George' and initialled it as an error.

Norah never married Dudley but lived with him from around the time of Tony's birth, changing her name by Deed Poll in 1928 to Elam, when Tony would have been about six years old.[165] Norah was obviously a woman with feminist and (by this time in her life) atheist convictions, such that her not getting married to Dudley may have been a clear choice the couple made to disregard social convention. However, when Sylvia Pankhurst chose this path in life her family were horrified, suggesting that the feminism represented by the former WSPU cadre did not extend to accepting unmarried couples with illegitimate children.

Given that Norah covered up her marital status by changing her name, it is more likely that not marrying was a choice forced on her and Dudley by their respective spouses who had refused to divorce. It may have also have been too financially damaging for Dudley to divorce, given that Dudley and Norah could be proven to be the adulterous parties, having had a child together. By using the name Elam, Norah clearly needed to give the appearance of social conventionality such that the majority of their acquaintances believed them to be married. This would not have fooled Grace Roe or Christabel Pankhurst, but it may well have fooled the Mosleys who they became friends with later on. The name change by Deed Poll may also have been necessary for some formal purpose such as the need to get Tony into a religious school or Norah's plans for taking charge of family affairs when her father died (which he did a few months later).

Norah and Dudley's relationship and the birth of an illegitimate child no doubt caused a great deal of unhappiness for Dudley's first family. Eustace, Dudley's oldest son, is recorded less than a month after Tony's birth as leaving London on 5 June 1922 on board SS Ballarat bound for Adelaide, Australia.[166] Eustace was 16 years of age, and described himself as a farmer. Eustace returned to England twice over the following years, once in 1930 from Australia[167] and then in 1947 from South Africa.[168] On the second occasion he arrived on board the steamship Durham Castle with his wife Elsie and two children, son Robin and daughter Jill, and went to stay with his mother, Ada, at 13 St Stephens Gardens, East Twickenham, where she had been living from at least 1922 when Tony was born.

Although Tony knew almost nothing about Norah and Dudley's wider family or previous spouses, he had been told about an elder half-brother. However, the story given by Norah and Dudley was that this brother had been involved in fraud, embezzlement and criminal activity, and they had paid him to leave the country and never return because of the shame he brought on them. It seems unlikely that a 16 year old boy could have behaved in such a way, and it seems more likely, given the timing of his departure, that he had been distraught by his parents' separation and his father having had an illegitimate child.

Dudley's daughter Carina got married in 1923[150] not long after the birth of Norah and Dudley's child. The marriage certificate suggests that Dudley was not present. In old age, Ada went to live with her daughter Carina and son-in-law Mr Wheatley. Ada died in 1962[169] 40 years after Dudley had left her, yet Ada is described on her death certificate as 'widow of Dudley Elam, a Clergyman'. The shame and upset that Ada and Dudley's children must have felt when he left them to live with his lover and illegitimate son must have been overwhelming for this to be how they felt they had to describe their mother when she died 40 years after the material events.

Clearly Dudley's family saw his behaviour as a betrayal, and some of the lies and deceit that were occasioned by Norah and Dudley's behaviour had a lasting effect on Dudley's new family as well. Norah was always the dominant partner in her and Dudley's relationship, and knowing how their lives developed from that point onwards, there can be little doubt that Norah demanded that Dudley leave his wife and family to support her, and that with his introverted, solitary, weak character, he gave way to her demands. Norah for her part always tried to 'big' Dudley up. Norah told her grandchildren that Dudley had been a very famous and brilliant Oxford don, but that they had not married because she was a feminist and marriage would have put her in subjection to her husband. Norah never spoke to Tony, his wife, or her grandchildren about Charles, her husband, and gave little information about Dudley's first family; all that was given were hints and derogatory explanations, leading Tony and his family to believe they were not worthy of consideration. The important relatives were Dudley's ancestors, who were always feted as illustrious royalty who should be looked, and lived, up to. Norah also never spoke of her birth family with her son or grandchildren. Norah's behaviour towards the Dohertys, her political activity, and the disgrace of her separation from her first husband and subsequent pregnancy may all have contributed to this. Other than that one of her brothers committed suicide, which Norah said was down to John Doherty's cruelty as a father, all that is known about her wider family has been established through genealogical research.

After the birth of their child, Norah and Dudley set up home with the baby at The Old Forge, Northchapel, Sussex. 'Nanny Pannell' was employed to look after Tony by Dudley who became quite concerned at Norah's inability to cope with motherhood. Ironically, Norah seemed to have become the personification of the bad suffragette portrayed in anti-suffragette media such as the postcard of a crying baby with the caption 'Mommy's a suffragette'. Mrs Pannell was originally employed part time, but she became concerned about leaving Norah alone with the baby as she would come back from time off to find mother and baby in a terrible state unable to complete basic tasks such as nappy changing. Mrs Pannell decided to take over full time care of the baby and Tony came to regard her as his mother; in fact it was not until he was nine years old that he realised that Norah was his mother.[31] Tony became very much an unwelcome nuisance in Norah's life and Nanny Pannell was therefore an important figure in Tony's young life, such that he remained in contact with her in adulthood, even taking the time to visit her with his wife and children before their emigration to South Africa in 1961 after Norah's death.

Mummy's a Suffragette.

Postcard, 1909 © Museum of London

Mr & Mrs Norah Elam

Although Norah became to a large extent estranged from her own family, the 1920s saw the death of her mother and then her father which kept her in the family sphere, albeit acrimoniously. Of Norah's siblings her two older stepsisters were Mary Ada and Emily Alice. Mary Ada had married Herbert Sands (a post office worker) in March 1891 while the family were living at Greenlands, Fairfax Road, Teddington, and she appears on the 1891 census as living with Herbert at her parent's home. Sadly, Mary Ada was to die two years later from tuberculosis.[170] According to the death certificate she died at Greenlands, and Charlotte, recorded on the certificate as her mother, was noted as being present. In reality Charlotte was Mary's stepmother, but it seems that the two had become close and that Charlotte chose to nurse Mary at home, a brave thing to do as tuberculosis was a highly infectious disease for which there was no cure at that time, and 50% or more of victims died.

Given John Doherty's known sensitivity to the death of his first wife, the subsequent death of her first born daughter may have fuelled more of the suppressed anger that seems to have been a such feature of his own temperament. Certainly, it seems that this was another event never talked about within the family as Norah never mentioned Mary Ada or her mother. Descendants of

Frank's family knew only vague details of a rumoured first marriage by John Doherty, and wrongly supposed that this had ended in divorce.

Emily Alice married Captain Augustus Pinto-Leite in London in 1901, and returned with him to live in South Africa in 1909 shortly after Norah's marriage to Charles Dacre Fox. Augustus held the rank of Trumpeter in the Natal Police and had been wounded at Laydysmith in 1900. He was presumably on long leave visiting relatives when he and Emily married in 1901.[171] At about this time Emily began calling herself Dorothy Pinto-Leite, identifying herself by this name on the outgoing ship's register. The couple returned to the UK in March 1919[172] aboard the steamship Durban Castle and from then on remained in the UK.

During the 1920s and 1930s Emily remained in close contact with Norah and they became joint executors of their father's estate in 1929. Emily's activities during this period are dominated by her commitment to animal welfare and anti-vivisection causes, a passion she and Norah obviously shared. During this period Emily is described as a 'leading light' in Our Dumb Friends' League[173] as well as other animal welfare organisations.

In 1931, Emily appears as a witness at a trial concerning a disturbance at an RSPCA meeting,[174] stating in evidence that she had been a member since January 1931. The matter was reported in the Guardian[175] and revolved around demonstrations carried out at an RSPCA AGM during which a Mr MacGregor was allegedly assaulted. The description in the Guardian of the factions in the RSPCA is noteworthy. The Counsel for the RSPCA described the Society as having two sections; 'the left wing or extreme section, and the other the right wing, or moderate section'. The extremists were apparently '100% animal' objecting to 'performing animals and that kind of thing' while the moderates 'confine themselves to beasts of burden being cruelly used'. Emily apparently gave evidence in support of Mr McGregor, one of the so-called 'extremists', indicating quite clearly where her sympathies lay. The following year in March 1932[176] Emily and her husband were ejected from a London cinema, where they had joined the audience and in the middle of the film Emily had stood up and disrupted proceedings by shouting 'I protest against this film'. Her explanation to newspaper reporters afterwards was that the public did not understand how animals were abused during training for film making.

In 1935 Emily again appears in legal proceedings to do with what the Guardian describes as "Civil War" between various factions of the British Union for the Abolition of Vivisection (BUAV).[177] Again Mr MacGregor is involved, claiming that he had been illegally expelled from the BUAV. The case revolves around Mr MacGregor's 'extreme' views being too forcefully expressed. In part he believed that the BUAV should not be associated with the RSPCA, an organisation which at that time had members that took part in field sports. He saw these activities as incompatible with animal welfare.

During the 1920s and 1930s Emily was a frequent visitor at Norah's home, The Old Forge in Northchapel, where she was known as Dotty, the aunt who had a pet monkey who would accompany her on her visits.[13] Emily treated the monkey like a child, sitting it up to the table to eat, and making it use the toilet.

This obsession with monkeys continued all of Emily's life. In 1945 Emily was awarded the Silver Medal of the Zoological Society of London (ZSL)[178] for her work in nursing sick chimpanzees. When the head keeper became ill, Emily took over nursing duties in the dedicated chimp nursery. The animals had contracted influenza, which Emily apparently succumbed to and was herself very ill for some time. These particular facilities were closed in 1953 when the chimps' nursery was moved to the care of dedicated keepers in the monkey house. However, Emily had kept hold of her key to the monkey house[179] and would regularly visit the zoo and let herself into the monkey house causing difficulties for the keepers. The matter came to light when she followed her usual practice and one of the monkeys bit her, at which point she was asked to return her key. It seems that her love of chimps was such that in December 1957, she was quoted in 'Table Talk by Pendennis' in the Guardian[180] under 'Sayings of the Week' as stating 'I only know about apes'.

Norah did not enjoy close or regular contact with any of her five brothers except Frank. At the time of Frank's marriage to Nellie Tozer, he was not living in the Doherty household, but at a house a short distance from it opposite Nellie's family home.[13] John Doherty did not attend Frank's wedding to Nellie, but Norah signed in his place. There were difficulties between Frank and John Doherty owing to some personal financial problems that seem to have been a regular feature of Frank's life. After the marriage Frank and Nellie began a new life in Canada. Frank sailed on the Teutonic to New York in 1909[181] and was joined by Nellie a year later. Four children were born to the couple in Canada, but only Frank and John survived to adulthood.

Redmond left Britain to settle in Australia around 1906 where he worked as a 'Horse Driver'. On his death he was unmarried and donated his body to the University of Sydney medical school, which would probably have provoked Norah's displeasure given her anti-medical establishment views. He died in Sydney on 5 June 1940 at the age of 67 years, having lived there for 34 years.[182] He was laid to rest on 21 February 1941 when the medical school released his body to a Roman Catholic cemetery for burial. As far as is known, Redmond never returned to the United Kingdom, but clearly kept in touch with his family as he sent flowers to both his mother's funeral in 1924 and his father's in 1929, although was not recorded as being present at either.[35,36]

The remaining two brothers emigrated to the USA; Hugh sailed for New York in 1911[183] with his wife Violet. Maurice, a furniture designer, sailed to New York in 1912, his wife Violet and daughter Lilian following 1913, and the family settled in Michigan.[184] He served in the US army in WWI.[185]

Hugh returned regularly to the United Kingdom probably in connection with his work. By 1927 he, Violet and Eileen, their only daughter, had re-settled permanently in London. In 1927 Violet was granted a divorce on the grounds of Hugh's adultery and was awarded custody of Eileen by the court together with a maintenance settlement.[186]

John Doherty Junior was the oldest son of John and Charlotte Doherty who remained in the UK. At first he worked in his father's printing business[32] but by the time of his father's death he was no longer working there. Sadly, he died in 1930 less than six months after his father from turberculosis of the larynx and exhaustion, and must have already been very ill at his father's funeral.[187]

Neal the youngest son; stayed in the UK, married, served in the British army in WWI[188] and attended his father's funeral in 1929. Neal experienced considerable financial difficulty during his working life, going through bankruptcy proceedings twice. The first time was in 1926, when proceedings were triggered by an unpaid tailoring bill,[189] and was released from this bankruptcy in 1928.[190] He and his wife Dorothy then set up a dairy farming business, but in 1928 that business collapsed. This time Dorothy was declared bankrupt[191] only being released from this bankruptcy in 1932.[192]

It seems that Frank returned to the UK shortly after his father's death,[193] having been sent a telegram by Norah telling him to come, yet if he was aiming to get to the funeral, he missed it by three months.[13] It is not known if any other family members in America were similarly summoned.

Norah's mother, Charlotte Isabel, had died five years earlier in May 1924, but strangely, a few months before John died in 1929 an *In Memoriam* notice appeared in The Times for Charlotte reading 'In unfading memory of Charlotte Isabel Doherty, for 50 years the dear wife and wise help of John Doherty of Longford Lodge, Hampton, who's long, useful, unselfish life ended on 2 May 1924'.[194] If John treated Charlotte as badly as Norah claimed, then this epitaph could not have been written by him, and one wonders whether Norah arranged for this obituary to be printed to irritate her father and avenge her mother in a small way given that her father was very ill and close to death by this time. It was after all Norah who had the experience of using the Times as a conduit for her views and opinions. It seems odd that John would have arranged such an obituary himself so long after his wife's death when he was 80 years old and very ill with throat cancer.

John Doherty died three months later in August 1929[195] having outlived his wife by just over five years. His funeral was detailed in The Times[196] as follows: 'List of Chief Mourners - Mr & Mrs John Doherty (son & daughter-in-law), Mr Neal Doherty (son), Captain and Mrs Augustus Pinto-Leite (son-in-law and daughter), Mrs & Mrs Norah Elam (son-in-law and daughter)'. It may seem unusual for a fairly ordinary middle class family to have a family funeral detailed in this way in The Times, and along with the fact that the Elam couple are listed in a untraditional format 'Mr & Mrs *Norah* Elam', one wonders again if Norah had a leading hand in having this item appear in The Times.

The 1882 Married Women's Property Act gave women the right to own property either given to or acquired by them, rather than for that property to pass immediately into their husband's ownership. However, it was not until the 1925 Administration of Estates Act that the law was scrapped that allowed property to pass to the eldest son in the absence of a will. John apparently left no will and Norah and Emily took advantage of this relatively recent law to claim the right (as the eldest children) to become joint executors of their father's estate, which they were duly granted by the probate court. Norah would have been well aware of her rights to sue for the estate and to retain it, as long as she had Emily's consent as the eldest surviving child.

In August 1929, a document was filed at the Probate office[197] stating that John Doherty died intestate leaving an estate of £5,000. The document authorised the issue of 'Letters of Administration of all the Estate' to Emily Pinto-Leite of 58 Kensington Gardens and Norah Elam 'wife of Charles Richard Dacre Fox' of The Old Forge, Northchapel, Petworth in the county of Sussex as 'the lawful daughters and the two persons entitled to share in the estate'. A few days later a notice appeared in the Times[198] confirming that Norah and Emily had been appointed as Administrators of the Estate, asking for anyone with 'debts, claims or demands' against the Estate to send written particulars within two months to Godfrey

B Rush, the solicitor acting for Emily and Norah. It appears no claims were made and Norah and Emily divided the estate between themselves. Norah and Emily must have colluded to take control of their father's estate, and to divide the spoils between them, leaving their brothers out. Norah assumed sole control of the printing business.

Given John Doherty's attitudes towards women he might have been expected to have left his property to his sons, and being politically aware he must have understood the new inheritance laws and the consequences of not having a will. One might therefore speculate about why John Doherty left no will, and even to question whether he did write a will that Norah persuaded him to destroy when he was close to death and easy to manipulate, as she often spoke about wanting revenge on her father.[31]

One can only speculate about what the Doherty brothers may have made of Emily and Norah's behaviour, and wonder whether Frank's tardy visit to the UK was in an attempt to help his brothers wrestle back something of what they felt they may have been entitled to. Frank and Neal did contemplate a legal challenge to Norah and Emily's claims on their father's estate. An Affidavit was filed by Frank and Neal in 1930 in the High Court of Justice, Chancery Division in the matter of Pinto-Leite and Elam v Doherty. The Affidavit included two certificates in respect of Frank's appointment as a Commissioner of Oaths in Canada.[199] Their claim was either withdrawn or unsuccessful.

Norah always described her father as a bully that she hated, but we cannot know why she felt the need to punish her brothers in this way other than that she may have felt driven to assert her ultra-feminist convictions. No doubt Norah believed that a printing business might be useful to her not just in terms of generating an income, but also as a useful resource for her political campaigns. The business had, as we have seen, been used for printing campaign posters during her previous enemy alien campaign.

In spite of Norah's great oratory and written skills, she seems to have had no talent for business and financial matters, and subsequently ran the printing business into the ground. Unfortunately, the 1882 Married Women's Property Act also gave women the 'right' to be sued for bankruptcy, and Norah became subject to this law. Prior to 1882 her true husband Charles may have been liable for her debts. By 1931 the business was in trouble, and Norah filed for bankruptcy on 3 September 1931.[200] In November 1931 she was subject to a public hearing and did not apply for a discharge until March 1933,[201] which resulted in a discharge order in June 1933.[202] The London gazette is a Crown publication and publishes all bankruptcy notices. In all the London Gazette notices Norah is recorded as 'Norah Elam, a married woman carrying on business as John Doherty Printer at 51 Temple Chambers'. Her name was by law 'Norah Elam' by this time, and she was still a married woman, but she was not married to Mr Elam as implied, which supports the suspicion that the formalisation of her name may have been largely for the purposes of taking over the business, and may, therefore, have been part of a scheme she plotted out when she knew her father was close to death.

Bankruptcy in the 1930s carried significant consequences. Initially, creditors would obtain a judgment for debts totalling not less than £50. Failure to comply with this judgement would result in a Bankruptcy Notice being served, with failure to respond to this procedure being interpreted as an act of bankruptcy. Thereafter, a Receiving Order would be issued followed by an Order of Adjudication.[203] In Norah's case this was the Order recorded in the London Gazette in 1931. The bankrupt would have had to undergo public examination of all their affairs. All Norah's 'books' (accounting manuals from the business) would have had to be submitted for examination by an Official Receiver of the Board of Trade, and she would have had to appear in person to explain fully how and why the business failure occurred. This was a prolonged and thorough procedure, designed to ensure that no debtor could dispose of or hide any assets that could or should be used to discharge their debts. No bankrupt could be discharged from their bankruptcy unless and until they had appeared in person in open court. Even after an Order of Discharge had been granted, the individual could begin to acquire property, but could be disbarred from holding public office for specified periods of time. Norah no doubt kept her lack of talent for accounting secret from Oswald Mosley and others she worked with in the 1930s, but the information about her bankruptcy would have been easily accessible to authorities such as MI5.

THE GOOD BODY

Norah was a staunch anti-vivisectionist and opponent of vaccination throughout her life. Although largely politically inactive during the 1920s, she continued to support the causes arguably closest to her heart associated with animal welfare, primarily through her membership of the London & Provincial Anti-Vivisection Society (LPAVS). This organisation campaigned not only on an anti-vivisection ticket, but was also opposed to vaccination, which it wholeheartedly condemned and campaigned against.

The LPAVS was founded in 1876,[204] and it is likely that Norah was a member from early on in her career. From 1919 Norah held the position of Honorary Secretary of the Society, serving on the Executive Committee, and from 1938 took on the additional responsibilities of Secretary and Editor.[205] Dudley joined the Executive Committee in 1935.[206] Among their fellow activists on the Executive Committee was Dr Bertrand P Allinson MRCS LRCP who served as Honorary Treasurer.[204] Dr Betrand Allinson was the son of Dr TR Allinson, the well known eugenicist, anti-vaccinationist and wholemeal bread manufacturer,[207] who was a founder member of Allied Bakeries. Both father and son were well known and prominent vegetarians, with Dr Bertrand

Allinson also being a member and serving on the Executive Committee of the London Vegetarian Society.

Inoculation for smallpox had been introduced into England from the East in 1716, and would be carried out by rubbing material from a smallpox pustule into a scratch between the thumb and forefinger. The recipient would develop a mild dose of smallpox which reduced the level of scarring and mortality, and for survivors gave immunity to the disease. By 1796 a safer method of inoculation had been developed by Edward Jenner who had developed a vaccine from the cowpox virus, which was non-fatal to humans, but induced immunity to smallpox. The original form of smallpox inoculation, therefore, fell into disuse and was finally banned in England in 1840, when vaccination became the Government's preferred disease control mechanism.

In 1853 Parliament passed a Compulsory Vaccination Act. Victorian vaccinators carried out their task using a lancet (a surgical instrument) to 'cut lines into the flesh in a scored pattern………. in at least four different places on the arm' which were then smeared with vaccine matter, also called lymph. Although calf lymph was available from the National Vaccine Establishment, government pressure resulted in public vaccinators keeping the supply flowing by vaccinating from arm to arm. After eight days babies who had been vaccinated were required to be made available so that lymph could be 'harvested' from their blisters, and applied to the next cohort. Fines were imposed on parents who did not cooperate.[207]

Durbach describes this procedure as '.....invasive, unsanitary, and sometimes disfiguring........being potentially more harmful than beneficial', and describes how, as a result, the 1853 Act became a catalyst for a highly charged public debate over vaccination. From the 1860s onwards public resistance grew with the anti-vaccination lobby seeking to have the 1853 Act repealed. The level of public protest and a highly politicized campaign meant that amendments were introduced to the 1853 Act in 1867 and 1871 to try and strengthen the law and enforce compliance levels. However, resistance remained high and by 1898 the Government proposed a compromise by introducing a clause into the legislation allowing conscientious objectors to vaccination to apply to a magistrate for a certificate of exemption, thus excusing individuals from the heavy fines imposed for non-compliance. Even this initiative failed and eventually in 1907 a new Vaccination Act was approved by Parliament.

The public debate was as much about the rights of the state to intervene and impose itself into an individual's personal life as it was about the efficacy of vaccination, and many prominent leaders of Victorian and Edwardian society harboured a dislike of medical intervention, belonging to societies opposed to scientific advancement through vivisection. Norah, like many leading women of her time had strong objections to the medical establishment and an affinity for 'natural' approaches to life and illness. The Theosophical Society, based on Eastern spirituality and spiritual healing attracted many Victorian and Edwardian women; Annie

Besant who became President of that society had also been an important figure in women's suffrage as a member of the NUWSS. Other leading women involved in the women's movement, including Nancy Astor, turned to Christian Science. Christian Science was also founded by a woman Mary Baker Eddy who practiced divine healing and proclaimed that all illness derived from the 'denial of God'. Christian Scientists refused medical interventions along with various other religious or spiritual organizations of the time. Lady Redesdale, the mother of the Mitford sisters, became well known for her views on how 'The Good Body' cures itself, and refused to accept medical interventions for her children; Christabel Pankhurst became a Seventh Day Adventist.

Between 40% and 60% of the leaders of this anti-medicine, anti-vivisection movement were women, and the support from the middle and upper class women in organisations without overtly female objectives was high.[208] Women were specifically excluded from scientific education during this period, and this helped to build up female resentment towards a male medical establishment that excluded women and actively worked to prevent them joining it. Added to this were Victorian and Edwardian social mores which left women feeling humiliated when having to confide intimate details or undress in front of male doctors. Anti-vivisection and anti-vaccination agitation gave these frustrations an outlet and allowed women to express themselves through activities like writing articles for in-house periodicals or writing to local newspapers, organising and demonstrating.

Many suffragettes held heterodox views on medical issues such as vaccination and as already noted many leading members of the suffrage movement became active in heterodox organisations such as anti-vaccination leagues, vegetarian societies, anti-vivisection societies, the Theosophical Society and Christian Science.

The WSPU and other suffragists clashed infamously with Sir Almroth Wright, a leading bacteriologist working on a new inoculation for typhoid. On 28 March 1912 the third Parliamentary Franchise (Women) Bill (known more commonly as the third Conciliation Bill) was due to be debated in the House of Commons. On the same day Sir Almroth Wright, in a letter to the Times, set out a virulent diatribe against suffragists, claiming that they were immoral, unbalanced, unreasonable and hypersensitive and that they suffered in excess from the afflictions of their sex generally in that that all women eventually and inevitably became insane because it was part of their nature and could not be avoided. The letter contained much more in a similar vein, claiming to be based on scientific medical evidence and set out the argument that women should be kept out of public life and confined to the home. This sparked a fierce debate between suffragists and anti-suffragists in the letter columns of the Times between 28 March 1912 and 17 April 1912. It is hardly surprising, therefore, that if Sir Almroth was representative of even a small section of the medical profession, women like Norah would have little time for his views on vaccination.

Former suffragettes who had clashed with Wright in 1912 would have remembered him well when they clashed with him again as anti-vaccinationists. Wright, as head of the Inoculation Department at St Mary's Hospital London in 1914, had been trying to persuade the Government to introduce compulsory inoculation against typhoid for British troops with a vaccine he had recently been trialling for widespread use. In this instance he failed to get Government on his side, yet the debate stirred the anti-vaccinationists, and during the period just after the outbreak of war another heated debate took place in the letter columns of The Times in which Wright expressed extreme and provocative views on the matter.[209]

The LPAVS was a non-charitable unincorporated society producing a monthly magazine 'The Animals' Guardian' subtitled 'A Humane Journal for the Better Protection of Animals', selling for 2d and edited by Charles W Forward. The contents were mostly factual articles covering issues such as anti-hunting, criticism of the use of animals in warfare, and condemnation of medical research using animals.[210]

The LPAVS had as its objects 'to secure the total abolition by law of the practice commonly called 'Vivisection' in which is included the inoculation of animals for experimental purposes, and to advocate the humane treatment of animals generally'. Although mainly concerned with animal welfare, anti-vaccination was a clear secondary object given that vaccinations were developed and safety tested through animal experimentation. Indeed in 1951, LPAVS published a pamphlet by Norah's colleague and leading opponent of vaccination, Dr Beddow Bayly, on 'The Relationship of Germs to Disease'. Norah had known Beddow Bayly since at least 1934 when he was reported in the LPAVS Annual Report and Accounts as a 'medical patron'. Norah was firm in her anti-vaccination stance all her life; refusing to have her son vaccinated and preventing him from having her grandchildren vaccinated in the early 1950s when they lived with her.

Using her experience for organising public meetings and giving speeches, in March 1921 Norah advertised[211] and chaired a public meeting of LPAVS to discuss 'The Dog's Bill' (Bill to prohibit the vivisection of Dogs) that was being debated in Parliament at that time. The meeting was held at Aeolian Hall in London and as Chair, Norah read out 20 letters from Members of Parliament in support of the bill, and stated that, 'A large majority of the public were strongly in favour of the measure, and she felt sure that victory would be theirs if a determined effort were made, especially if women made proper use of their new political power'.[212] This could have been the start of her next major campaign, had she not fallen pregnant and moved away from London. Prevented from being publicly active on the London scene, Norah devoted much time to studying and gathering information which was to culminate in her writing two monographs attacking the Medical Research Council and the medical establishment.

As a precursor to this Norah had gathered a wealth of information previously when, during 1916 and 1917, she had worked part time supervising a typewriting pool at the Medical Research Council (MRC). In 1916, Waldorf Astor MP was the Chairman of the MRC. His wife Nancy Astor had been involved with Mrs Pankhurst's work during WW1, and Norah had worked with Nancy Astor in Plymouth when they jointly organised a talk given by Mrs Pankhurst. It seems possible that through this link to the Astors, Norah had obtained a brief spell of work at the MRC as a supervisor of the typewriting staff preparing the 1916-17 Annual Report.[213] Norah did not remain long in this job[214] and even while she was doing this work she was no doubt prioritising her campaign work on the enemy alien peril, which would have kept her very busy. Given her enduring distrust of doctors, a lifelong commitment to the welfare of animals and strong anti-vaccination stance, it seems likely that she took this job primarily to gain inside information on the MRC.

The Medical Research Committee, renamed the Medical Research Council in 1918, had been brought into being in 1913, and arose out of the initiative of the then Liberal Government which brought in the National Insurance Act of 1911 during the period when Lloyd George was Chancellor of the Exchequer. This was part of the social welfare reforms started by that Government which are now regarded as forming the basis of our modern welfare state. In 1913 funds were provided under the National Insurance Act to create a single medical research organisation for the whole of the United

Kingdom, which would undertake wide ranging extensive medical research, not restricted to tuberculosis.

An annual report was produced by the MRC addressed to the Chairman of the National Health Insurance Joint Committee to be laid before Parliament giving '……an account ….. of the research work which has been organised by the Committee and supported by grants from the Medical Research Fund in the past year'. During the war years the report was split into two parts; the first part examined ongoing medical research topics from before the start of the war including tuberculosis, rickets and heart disease; the second part dealt with research that had been commissioned specifically in connection with, and as a result of, the war, such as treatment of infected wounds, trench nephritis, dysentery, industrial fatigue and the health of munitions workers.

In 1934 and 1935 the LPAVS published two companion-piece monographs written by Norah: 'The Vitamin Survey, A Reply'[215] and 'The Medical Research Council, What it is and how it works'[216] in which she pummelled the MRC. In 1932 the Medical Research Council had produced a paper called 'Vitamins, A Survey of Present Knowledge'. Norah's 'Reply' in 1934 was a critical appraisal of that survey and its results. To undertake the writing of her paper, Norah had to embark on an extensive survey of the research into vitamins up to that point and to understand many of the technical research explanations given in medical papers. To that extent Norah fulfilled her own brief very well, illustrating through her arguments that she understood and could argue her side in the technical issues and jargon.

Norah's second paper 'The Medical Research Council' was based on the same arguments about MRC research practices and remits, but distilled and argued more cogently on a broader front, even if full of her usual rhetoric. Norah argued that the MRC was a costly luxury for the country, funded by the taxpayer, which was totally undemocratic. Her argument was that 'powerful vested interests' had managed to 'entrench' themselves behind 'State-aided research', and had managed to make themselves unaccountable; the public were unable to influence the decisions about what research should be undertaken, and it operated like a closed shop, only answerable to itself.

Norah also argued that the research carried out involved the cruel and inhumane use of animals, and that any thinking person had to question how and why research and results based on animal models could safely be extrapolated to humans. Finally, she complained that animal experimentation was doubly cruel because of the unnecessary repetition of experiments to replicate or prove the same point, which in many cases she argued could have been arrived at by simple, common sense. In the case of vitamins, research had been based on trying to identify individual vitamins and understand diseases caused by particular vitamin deficiencies, when all that was needed was to ensure that if everyone got a good, varied diet, no one would have dietary deficiencies.

What does it matter what we call the property or substance (ie Vitamin) so long as we are satisfied that fresh vegetables and fruits can both prevent and cure a condition of ill-health which results from lack of them?...In the case of each vitamin presented to us, we have found that where reliance has been placed on animal experiments, the theories evolved have been both misleading and dangerous, but that where that reliance has been based upon clinical observation on man, the theories are sound and reasonable, and scientific facts are demonstrated.[215]

Although Norah had no relevant education in medical research methods, she clearly felt sufficiently passionate about the issue that she educated herself in the technical issues and jargon and was able to put forward a strong case which could stand up to the medical expertise of the time, much of which remains relevant today.

In addition to researching and producing these pamphlets, during 1931 and 1932 Norah also undertook two extensive road campaigns for the LPAVS, touring extensively in Nottingham, Derbyshire, Yorkshire, Bedfordshire, and Huntingdonshire, holding meetings in all the main cities.[204] In 1931 Norah apparently toured in a motor van, but in 1932 for practical reasons connected with the 'necessarily cumbrous nature' of the motorvan, undertook the tour 'with her own small car which, decorated with posters, and with the addition of a portable platform, proved an admirable rallying-point for interested audiences'.

At the outbreak of war her association with the LPAVS gained the organisation widespread notoriety due to Norah and some of her fellow anti-vivisectionists (including Mary Allen) also being members of Oswald Mosley's British Union of Fascists. This led to the secret services being concerned about the organisation and believing it was a front for fascist activities. However, while the organisation may have given Norah a vehicle to pursue or legitimise some of her fascist activities, there is no doubt that she held very strong beliefs about anti-vivisection and cruelty to animals and the temptation to try to combine activities for both organisations by her and her colleagues helped lead to the suspicions of MI5. Certainly the fact that Norah was always known within LPAVS circles as Dacre Fox, despite changing her name to Elam in 1928, and was then known in BUF circles by both names, must have muddied the waters or added to MI5's suspicions, particularly since, as we shall see, they were unsure as to Norah and Dudley's married status.

Far from being a front for anything, a love of animals was the single most consistent aspect of Norah's character, lasting her whole life. As a child Norah had intervened to try and prevent her father from whipping his dogs and had received a lash across the face in the process.[31] In some ways she cared more for animals than she did for people and this became particularly true in her old age when her dearest companion was a pedigree daschund called Maximillian who slept under the covers at the bottom of her bed. Norah spoiled Max and treated with him more kindness and thought than any human in her life, including her son and grandchildren. When Max disappeared one day an extensive frantic search was made of the grounds of Gothic Cottage, and Norah was desperately upset and worried when he could not be found. Some days later Max was found dead in the grounds of the cottage, poisoned. Norah believed he had been killed deliberately, was distraught at the way he died, and tormented by the unnecessary pain he suffered. She spent several solitary days languishing in the garden pining and grieving for Max and becoming increasingly hostile and menacing to her family.

Norah's distrust of science also extended to every day encounters, and being willing to campaign on anything she felt strongly about. Norah once went uninvited and unceremoniously to a local margarine factory, where she witnessed the workers sloshing around in gumboots in the margarine that people were going to eat. Norah described the conditions as 'insalubrious and disgusting',[31] and claimed that the chemical ingredients used to produce margarine were the same as the oils used in cars and vehicles, referring to it as 'axle-grease'. On ordering a scone with butter in a tea-shop once, Norah was brought margarine instead, at which she made a characteristic outburst, refusing to pay, and left the establishment leaving them in no doubt as to her views on the matter.[31]

Fascism Next Time

The interwar years saw two General Elections in 1931 and 1935, both dominated by issues arising out of The Great Depression, which had engulfed governments worldwide in a financial crisis that caused difficulties in balancing national budgets, arguments about free trade versus protectionism, poverty and general hardship. The general crisis in government that this brought meant that Britain opted for two coalition National Governments.

West Sussex Blackshirts

While Norah was busy tying up her father's estate, dealing with bankruptcy and studying medical research for her campaign against the MRC, Dudley was working for the West Sussex branch of the Conservative Party and Tony was being looked after by Nanny Pannell while also receiving education at a local boarding school.

Dudley was appointed to the General Purposes and Finance Committee of the West Sussex Conservative Association in April 1929[217] and served until April 1934, when his resignation is recorded in the Minutes. Dudley was a minor figure in this local branch of Conservatives, and was never the Chairman as later claimed in Fascist Press; the Chairman for most of the period being Captain Weller-Poley.

Dudley was a reliable fastidious attender, and over six years appears to have missed only five monthly meetings. His roles in the organisation appear mundane and inconsequential. In 1930 and 1931 he was the Sussex delegate to special conferences and meetings held in London. In March 1931 he was appointed to a Leaflet Subcommittee (to campaign to Head Office on the 'pathos and patriotic appeal' of election leaflets). In 1932 and 1933 he served as a member of the Finance Sub-Committee and in 1932 was an elected delegate to the South Eastern Advisory Committee and the Council of the Sussex Provincial Division.

Norah was also a member of the Conservative Party in spite of her former and later objections to party politics, though she seems to have been a fairly inactive member with virtually no information coming to light about any public activities. The only recorded instance of her giving a talk to a Conservative Party meeting was in November 1933 in Plaistow at Winterton Hall, which Dudley reported on briefly at the Chichester committee; this information being recorded in the minutes of the Chichester Conservative Committee.

Meanwhile, Oswald Mosley, a brilliant, handsome, young, titled and wealthy politician had been looking set for a brilliant career in politics. He had been elected as a

Conservative MP at the age of 21 in the 1918 election but had crossed the floor after falling out with the Tory party over their policy concerning the Black and Tans in Ireland, an issue also close to Norah's heart. Mosley then allied with the Left and hoped to gain a position in the 1929 Labour government. Dissatisfied with his progress in the Labour Party, he formed the New Party based on economic reform policies, but failed to win a seat in the 1931 election. Although the New Party initially attracted some solid Labour members such as Aneurin Bevan, after losing the election in 1931 Mosley's economic policies became more fascist in orientation. In 1931 Mosley created the British Union of Fascists (BUF), and in 1933 Hitler was elected to power in Germany. Mosley would inevitably be an attractive figure to Norah, having the thoroughbred social status she fantasised about Dudley having and with the dynamic political career that she herself desired.

Oswald Mosley had begun an affair with Diana Guinness (formerly Mitford) in 1932 and Diana's sister Unity Mitford, although banned by her father from associating with Mosley, met Mosley that same year and joined the BUF. Norah claimed to have had a close friendship with Unity and Diana which predated her joining the BUF,[31] but although she probably began associating with the BUF from its inception in 1931, it seems that she formally joined the organisation in 1934 along with Dudley. Norah would have prized a friendship with two young attractive socialites, regaining her place in respectable society, even allowing herself to be referred to occasionally as 'Lady Dacre Fox'.

Although she no doubt regaled them with tales of her suffragette days, she kept her current marital status a secret and probably never mentioned her son.

Although it is unknown exactly when Norah met Mosley for the first time, there are a number of times when she may have taken notice of him in his previous political career. Norah and Mosley both spent some time with Nancy Astor[218] and may have encountered each other through Nancy's wide and active social set. Mosley stood in the 1918 General Election campaigning on the enemy alien issue which may have brought him into contact with Norah. Around 1920-1921 Mosley also took a firm stance against the government on the Black and Tans policy which would have appealed to Norah. However, while Norah may have been aware of Mosley during these periods, it seems more likely that she did not meet him until after the BUF was formed, since while Mosley was aware of her suffragette past and her former marriage, he seems to have been unaware that she was not actually married to Mr Elam. If she was as she claimed close friends with Unity and Diana Mitford it seems likely that she could have met Mosley through this connection.

Unity and Diana first visited Germany in 1933 when they attended the fifth Nuremberg Rally. They did not meet Hitler during this visit, but visited several times after this from 1934 onwards and eventually met Hitler, who Unity in particular admired and became close to with many rumours about them having a close personal relationship. Norah would later claim that she had visited

Germany to meet Hitler with Unity along with a group of four or five other British women, but on the day it had rained and they had gone back to their hotel to change their clothes. When they returned, Hitler had been and gone.[31] If this story is true it would have happened between 1934 and 1938 before MI5 began recording Norah's activities, since there appears to be no record of Norah's visit in the MI5 files currently available which record many of her activities from 1938 onwards.

On deciding to join the BUF, Norah knew that she would have to persuade Dudley to join her and to leave the Conservatives behind. Rather than have Dudley leave quietly, Norah turned the move into a minor propaganda coup for the BUF by depicting Dudley as a significant Conservative defector (in spite of his relevant insignificance within the organisation) and publishing his resignation letter (which she undoubtedly wrote) in the Fascist Weekly.[219]

The letter complains that the Conservative Party had not worked in the National interest, but had '....consistently, from top to bottom, with a few exceptions, supported, voted and helped in every possible way, the subversive policy of the Socialist Prime Minister'. It complains of government policy toward India (a favourite topic of William Joyce, later known as 'Lord Haw Haw' who was then the BUF West Sussex Area Administrative Officer and, therefore, Norah's senior colleague) and talks of economic internationalism that is 'more dangerous and more insidious than Communism'. The letter ends, 'I prefer to go out into the wilderness and start the fight all over again, in the hope that I may see a new spirit regenerated in the National Interest, but this spirit can only lie by fighting for what is right, not by compromising with what is corrupt and evil'.

This letter sets the tone for Dudley and Norah's political activities within the BUF, and they wasted no time getting Norah back on a regular speaking platform where she would have felt most comfortable preaching her fierce logic. Although Norah had to be somewhat subjected to the masculinity of the BUF and become known as 'Mrs Dudley Elam' instead of 'Mrs Norah Elam', she was clearly the more dynamic one in the couple and was a far more prolific agitator, speaker and writer than her husband.

In April 1934 Norah shared her first platform at the Chichester Assembly Rooms with William Joyce.[220] At this point Joyce was a prominent and rising BUF activist, who was working full time for the organisation as the Director of Research and Director of Propaganda. Norah and Joyce would be working together given their prominent roles in the West Sussex Area until 1937 when Joyce fell out with Mosley. Shortly after this Norah and Dudley moved from West Sussex back to London. Although Norah's talent for propaganda and rhetoric may have drawn her to William Joyce, she disliked him intensely,[31] which may have been due partly to their very different views on Ireland, or may have come about when Joyce fell out with Mosley.

Norah's abiding interest in Irish affairs was conveyed to Tony in later years, when she would talk about how much she loathed the Black and Tans, and would frequently laugh when relaying reports of their capture by local IRA fighters and their being 'strung up to lamp posts'. William Joyce on the other hand claimed to have been a young recruit to the Black and Tans.

The Black and Tans had been recruited by the British Government in 1920 as a paramilitary force employed under the wing of the Royal Irish Constabulary to help them suppress the nationalist Home Rule movement and revolution in Ireland. Its specific remit was to target the Irish Republican Brotherhood and the Irish Republican Army who were waging guerrilla war on the Royal Irish Constabulary, making it difficult to recruit and police remote rural areas within Ireland. The men who were recruited were largely former WW1 veterans who found it difficult to find employment post war, and the offer of very good wages (ten shillings a day), saw around 9,500 volunteer. They got their name from the uniforms they wore, and became known for their brutality and savagery in dealing with not only the IRA but with civilians as well. One of the more notorious incidents for which they were known was the massacre of 12 civilians at a football match taking place at Croke Park, Dublin, in November 1920. This was carried out in retaliation for the murder of 14 undercover detectives by the IRA, and in turn led to further violence and eventually saw the burning down of the centre of Cork by a Black and Tan auxiliary force.

William Joyce was born in New York in 1906 of an Irish catholic father and English protestant mother. His family returned to live in Galway when he was three, and during his adolescence he became a fanatical British patriot, running away from home to join the Black and Tans, although Martland reports that he was never a fully fledged member as they discovered he was too young to be signed up.[221] Once his identity as an informer for the Black and Tans became known, IRA threats against him meant he had to leave for England.

Joyce then studied in England before joining the BUF, but by 1937 found himself dismissed from the BUF by Mosley, at which point he formed the British National Socialist League. Shortly before a warrant was issued for his arrest in England in 1939, he travelled to Germany with his wife. He then gained a notorious reputation as Lord Haw Haw, broadcasting propaganda to Britain from Germany, and was eventually captured by British forces near the end of the war and hung in Wandsworth Prison in January 1946 after being found guilty of treason.

Although Norah disliked Joyce, she believed that his execution by the British in 1946 was wrong, stating that he should not have been regarded as a traitor to England because he was not English but Irish.[31] In fact, although Joyce's parents were born in Ireland, Joyce was an American citizen. The British authorities went to great lengths to be able to demonstrate Joyce's Englishness, adamant that he would not evade the charge of treason on grounds of nationality, and did so on the grounds that he held a British passport at the time that he left England for Germany.

Norah's idea of Joyce's Irish nationality (based on his parents' place of birth) fits with her WW1 stance against Germans living in Britain whereby she insisted that even naturalised Germans could not be truly loyal to England and remained German at their core. The idea of pure nationhood may help to explain her Irish nationalist tendencies displayed in her hatred of the Black and Tans and her fury at the Ulstermen's wish to separate Ireland. The consistent idea is one in which individuals somehow inherently belong to their country of origin and nations must remain pure and discreet. Yet what remains unexplained is that Norah espoused a fierce English patriotism while by her own logic she was truly Irish and could not be patriotic to England. Therefore, either Norah failed to apply her own logic to herself, or it is possible that her mother Charlotte Clarke was in fact born into an English family living in Ireland and that the Doherty's move to England was a move back to Charlotte's family. As a feminist, Norah would presumably find it easy to reconcile the idea of inherent nationality passing through the mother's line of descent rather than the father's.

With Joyce as Area Administrative Officer, Dudley as Sub-Branch Officer for Worthing[222] and Norah as Sussex Women's Organizer,[223] West Sussex became a hub of fascist activity. The BUF produced a Rule Book setting out its administration and organizational rules in one thoroughly comprehensive, regimented volume covering everything from financial rules, meeting organisation, and conditions of membership, through to the specific duties for the office holders. A Chief Woman Organizer would have to be trained and then take on training themselves, be available to undertake propaganda marches, street sales, literature distribution, mass canvassing, street collections, public speaking and generally do all they could to recruit new members through Ward meetings. Women were expected to be fully conversant with BUF policy and be able to hold her own answering questions about it.[224] Norah was clearly a busy woman.

In June 1934 Mosley held a mass rally at Olympia which marked a turning point for the BUF's public image.[218] The brutality at Olympia, and the subsequent street riots, eventually saw a Public Order Act passed in 1936, which banned the wearing of political uniforms. Public support for the BUF which had been growing since its formation in 1931 began to fall off. The immediate aftermath of Olympia saw the BUF lose the support of Lord Rothermere and his newspaper empire, while William Joyce, Norah's 'line manager' in the Sussex area, became Deputy Leader of the BUF taking the BUF into a more hard line anti-Semitic phase. It seems that Norah and Dudley had become active in the BUF just as it was turning from a potentially mainstream movement into a radical fringe party, much as Norah had joined the WSPU at the start of its descent into extreme militancy and the ensuing loss of public support.

In West Sussex, fascist activity organized by Joyce and the Elams ranged from rallying speeches, to summer camps, to lunches, to violent street brawls:

Blackshirt Camp Opened - The Blackshirt Summer Camp at West Whittering near Chichester, Sussex, was opened last Saturday. The first contingent was met by Mrs ED Elam, the Sussex County Women's Organiser, and her husband when they halted for lunch at Petworth.[225]

Mrs Dudley Elam, Area Organiser for Sussex and Hampshire held a very successful meeting at Littlehampton, addressing a crowd of over 100 people. She spoke for about an hour and gave a clear and lucid exposition of Fascist policy notwithstanding a certain amount of heckling form the Communist element in the audience.[226]

Sir Oswald Mosley, Leader of the British Union of Fascists, Mr William Joyce, Director of Propaganda, Charles Bentinck Budd, Area Officer for West Sussex and Bernard Mullins, appearing at Worthing police court to answer charges of alleged riotous assembly following a Blackshirt meeting were committed for trial...[227]

The incident leading to Mosley and Joyce being arrested and put on trial took place after a meeting at Pier Pavilion, Worthing on 9 October 1934. This meeting followed the pattern set by Olympia. Mosley, Joyce and the other men became involved in violent clashes with crowds before and after Mosley addressed an invited audience inside the Pavilion. The charges against them were of alleged riotous assembly, asserting that the four defendants had deliberately 'walked up and down outside the Pavilion and later in Warwick Street, and violently assaulted perfectly inoffensive and law-abiding citizens of Worthing'. Norah was present and was later called to give evidence on behalf of Mosley and his co-defendants. She stated that she had heard two women shouting about Mosley, 'Where is he? He is afraid to come out, he always does this. Let's spit on him.' Other witnesses had heard them chanting 'One! Two! Three! Four! Five! We want Mosley, dead or alive!'

William Joyce had particular ambitions beyond West Sussex, harbouring a desire to become Viceroy of India under a Mosley administration should he ever head a BUF government.[221] Joyce, therefore, took a particular stand against the government's India Bill. The Bill, which was eventually passed in 1935, was designed by the Government to give a measure of autonomy to India, allowing more freedom and the development of limited self-government. Joyce is recorded as describing the backers of the bill as 'feeble' and 'one loathsome, fetid, purulent, tumid mass of hypocrisy, hiding behind Jewish Dictators'. In the Blackshirt, the BUF adopts the same line, describing the Bill as a chance for financial interests to 'fleece' India and restore slavery. Joyce had the Elams work for him on this policy which saw Norah addressing a county meeting at Lodsworth near Midhurst[228] and Dudley giving a talk in Guildford,[229] the only speech Dudley is reported to have made.

Although Norah seemed to need Dudley by her side throughout her BUF career, Dudley himself was a relatively minor figure. He makes very few public contributions, and where he does, he seems to put intellectualism ahead of the dynamism and mass appeal needed for 1930s extreme politics:

> **Our Reader's Views - Dangers of Meddling : Jewish Exploitation of Road Workers**
>
> *Fascism v Democracy BC 427 - In reading again the 'Phaedrus of Plato' I have come across the following passage - 'Well then must there not be in those who are to speak meritoriously, an understanding well acquainted with the truth of the things they are to speak about?' 'Nay', answers Phaedrus (Baldwin & Co) 'It is this way I have heard about it: That it is unnecessary for anyone who would be a master of speech to learn what really is just, for instance: but rather what seems just to the multitude who are to give judgement: nor again what is good and beautiful: but only what seems so to them'. Comment is needless.*[230]

Dudley clearly did not feel the need to expound or explain his ideas with profuse rhetoric or to spell out his meaning to lay audiences. In further exhibition of his mundane significance, he sends a letter to Action:

> *Congratulations - I feel I must write to you to congratulate you most heartily on the enormous improvement in 'Action' and for the extra vim displayed also in the much improved makeup. E Dudley Elam.*[231]

Meanwhile, Norah's public speaking career in the BUF unsurprisingly gathers pace and is far from mundane:

> *The Basingstoke Groups held a social on the evening of 23 January to welcome Mr and Mrs Elam, Sussex and Hants Area Officers. The meeting was well attended by members and guests, and Mrs Elam made an excellent speech holding the attitude of her audience for an hour'.*[232]

> *Bognor Regis – a very busy week for propaganda for the National Peace Campaign culminated on Tuesday September 3 in a well attended meeting, very ably addressed by Mr Wegg-Prosser and our Women's Area Inspector, Mrs Elam. The audience was most interested and attentive.*[233]

> *Mrs D Elam gave a brilliant speech at Alton on Sunday and roused an apathetic audience with some startling information concerning the Covenant of the League.*[234]

> *Portsmouth and Southsea – dockyard meetings going strong. Increased local activity. Mrs Elam spoke at Unicorn Gates July 7 – very interested crowd.*[235]

> *Alton - Reds Deny Women Speakers Free Speech…Mrs Elam also addressed the audience but received the same treatment [as Mrs Muriel Whinfield].*[236]

> *Guildford – successful meeting at Village Hall, West Clandon. Mrs Elam spoke. Attendance nearly a hundred. Excellent literature sales.*[237]

November 1935 saw another General Election returning another National Government led by the Conservatives. Mosley did not put forward any candidates, choosing instead to campaign for voter abstention with the slogan 'Fascism Next Time'.[218] Norah campaigned for non-election in Worthing on a peace banner, asking '…..voters to get a definite assurance in writing from their candidate before voting, that he would not support any action likely to drag Britain into such a war. She herself had fought for the vote as a Suffragette and this is the first time that she was not going to use her vote. None of the old parties when they got to power had the machinery to tackle the vast problem of unemployment. Fascism alone provided the solution to overcome this evil, a solution which had never been challenged'.[238]

Being good loyal fascists, during the election campaign Dudley and Norah hung a huge banner across the entire frontage of The Old Forge with the slogan 'Fascism Next Time' in huge letters. If Dudley and Norah had not already made a mark on Northchapel by this time, they certainly drew plenty of attention to themselves with this unabashed declaration of their political affiliation. They then organized a rally at the Swan Inn Hall (now called The Deepwell Inn) about 200 yards up the road from the Old Forge. John Beckett addressed 'an enthusiastic audience' of members from neighbouring branches, and '..after the meeting, nearly 100 Blackshirts led by Mr Beckett under command of DO Hudson marched behind the standards to the Old Forge for refreshments at the invitation of Mr & Mrs

Elam.' Dudley and Norah kept a library of Fascist literature at The Old Forge, and would keep open house for anyone wanting to consult it, which no doubt made their home an appealing venue for post-rally refreshments.[239]

In November 1937 another meeting took place in Northchapel[240] where the prospective Parliamentary candidate for the area, Commander Hudson, was introduced by AK Chesterton, now editor of the Blackshirt and a leading propagandist for the BUF.

Rather than campaign in the 1935 election, Mosley prepared for the next election and in 1936 announced a list of BUF candidates for the following general election. Commander Hudson was clearly considered the best choice for Chichester and William Joyce was put forward for London County Council elections in 1937. Norah may have been disappointed not to be put forward for any areas she was familiar with, but she was put forward by Mosley, even if the proposed constituency was a long way from home. Norah clearly failed to disclose to Mosley that she had been bankrupt between 1931 and 1933 and although she was discharged from the bankruptcy, and was, therefore, allowed to stand for Parliament, it would have nonetheless carried a significant stigma and produced bad publicity for the BUF had she ever stood in a General Election and her bankruptcy been discovered. The news of Norah's candidacy for the Northampton seat was announced first in The Times[241] who published a list of the first twelve Fascist candidates.

Action gives a brief description of each of the twelve prospective candidates[242] describing Norah as :

Mrs Norah Elam – Was one of the leaders of the Woman's Suffrage Movement in pre-war days, served three terms of imprisonment and endured several hunger strikes. On the outbreak of hostilities she placed her services at the disposal of the Government. Mrs Elam had a distinguished war record - recruiting in 'Red' South Wales working in a munitions factory, and was a member of several important government committees. In 1918 she contested Richmond, Surrey, as an Independent candidate, was then for a short time in the Conservative Party, but joined the British Union almost at its conception. She is a popular and well known Fascist propagandist.

The claims are inevitably exaggerated and misleading. The reference to war work refers to the work with the Pankhursts calling on workers not to strike, and campaigning to allow women to work in the factories. Despite the inference that Norah worked in a munitions factory, there is no evidence at all to show that she did this, although it is possible she did speak in one during the Pankhurst campaign. The only 'important government committee' Norah ever served on was as typing pool supervisor for the MRC. Nevertheless, Norah had clearly impressed the BUF leadership sufficiently to win a nomination, while Dudley had so far made very little dent in Mosley's estimation. While Norah was given a parliamentary candidacy, Dudley was awarded a 'Bronze Award – a Birthday Honour for Distinguished Service by The Leader', on the fifth anniversary of the founding of the Union.[243]

Norah was described by a local Northampton newspaper as a strange candidature, occasioning 'initial surprise'.[244] The choice may also have been strange for Norah who had no obvious connections to the area, although she was probably familiar with Captain George Drummond, a friend of the Duke of Windsor, who was also a member of the London & Provincial Anti-Vivisection Society and a local Northamptonian who has latterly been identified as having supported the BUF.[245]

Mosley accompanied Norah to Northampton to introduce her to her electorate at a meeting in the Town Hall.[246] Mosley announced that 'He was glad indeed to have the opportunity of introducing the first candidate, and it killed for all time the suggestion that National Socialism proposed putting British women back into the home. Mrs Elam, he went on, had fought in the past for women's suffrage ..... and was a great example of the emancipation of women in Britain'.

Action and Blackshirt report Norah's speech at this meeting as a great success claiming that 'At the close of her speech I knew by the reception accorded to her that the people had taken her to their hearts'. The Northampton and County Independent, a local middle class weekly newspaper, was fairly relaxed about reporting on Norah's campaign and allowed her almost a whole page of the newspaper to write an election broadcast entitled 'Why I Am Contesting Northampton'.[244] Norah appealed to the inhabitants of this industrial town by speaking of unemployment, the failure of party politics and the resurrection of industry under a Fascist regime:

> *I shall ask them to arm me with their sovereign power to go in their name to Westminster, backed by their direct mandate, to change fundamentally and by constitutional means the system which has so lamentably failed…*
>
> *Moreover, [Northampton's] staple industry must, unless it is to perish as the staple industries in other areas have perished, turn for its very life to an economic system built on national rather than on international lines.*

Acknowledging that a vote for the BUF would be risky and unconventional, she appealed to what she claimed was a local progressive temperament to think radically and vote unconventionally, reminding them of a famous radical, Charles Bradlaugh who originated in Northampton, had supported women's suffrage, and worked with Annie Besant on various revolutionary projects. When elected to parliament in 1880 for Northampton, as an atheist he had requested a right to 'affirm' rather than take a religious oath of allegiance. He forfeited his seat and was imprisoned, yet at several subsequent by-elections the town consistently re-elected him:

> *From the time of Bradlaugh, when it refused to allow the House of Commons to interfere with its free decisions, it has shown a spirit of sturdy independence in keeping with British Union principles.* [244]

Norah gave a talk to the Northampton 'League of Nations Youth Group' who had been holding a series of meeting on 'Politics and World peace'.[247] Norah used this opportunity to tackle one of her favourite topics, which was to attack the League of Nations and the concept of collective security in favour of individual nations building their own Empire as far as they were able. This topic is discussed in more detail later. Norah was also given a further spread in the Northampton and County Independent to present the BUF policy on the Monarchy, which is one of the few times Norah talks about what Fascism stands for rather than what it stands against. Whether or not Norah had begun to make an impact on the middle classes of Northampton, she was to be disappointed a second time in seeking a seat in Parliament, as no election was called before the war.

The Old Forge, Northchapel 1935
Photograph by courtesy of the Friends of Mosley

Norah Elam, Candidate for Northampton 1936
Photograph by courtesy of Friends of Mosley

> FRIDAY. **Mercury & Herald**
>
> SIR OSWALD MOSLEY (right). With him are, left to right: Mr. G. C, Mr. Harry Frisby, and Mrs. Norah Elam, prospective Fascist candidate at Northampton.

Norah Elam with Oswald Mosley 1936
Northampton Mercury & Herald

The Old Forge, Northchapel 2009
Picture taken by Angela McPherson

OLD SUFFRAGETTE

Mosley became aware of Norah's talent for delivering propaganda effectively in speech and in print. As a former suffragette and feminist, Mosley saw an opportunity to employ Norah in a propaganda initiative to draw more women to the BUF and assist the BUF with its overly masculine image problem. Norah's writing career with the BUF, particularly as an 'old suffragette', was thus prolific In the Blackshirt, she had articles published on the 'Tragedy of Passchendale' (a response to Major Fuller's attack on WW1 Generals and their reliance on outdated war strategies), 'Fascism will Mean Real Equality: By an old Suffragette' (an anonymous article but undoubtedly penned by Norah) and 'Suffragette in Anti-Fascist Circus: Flora Drummond Tries Bluffing the Women' (an attack on Flora Drummond's Women's Guild of Empire, a right-wing league opposed to communism and fascism). In Action she wrote 'A Great Illusion - Poison Gas and Poison Tongues', 'Women and the Vote', a book review of 'A False Utopia' by William Chamberlin and 'J'Accuse - Failure of the Women's Movement'. Norah was also revered as one of the few female authors to be published in the intellectual journal of the fascist movement, Fascist Quarterly, in which she had two articles published on 'Women, Fascism and Democracy' and 'The Affirmative Guaranty'.

Although Norah wrote for propaganda purposes, there are some common themes which illuminate her past and present as a feminist political thinker. Her broad thesis which spins through her pen repeatedly is that as a former suffragette she had earned a moral authority to speak about women's freedom under democracy and that the freedom she helped to win was, she believed, a bluff. Democracy, she argued, had failed, was antiquated and worn out, and the Party system upon which democracy is based enslaves women and men alike. Her feminist themes are well-rehearsed, but she also theorises on other mainstream Fascist concepts including collective security and nation.

This 'Old Suffragette' vehemently claims her moral right to pronounce on matters relating to women's freedom given her own part in that battle. Norah was evidently goaded into writing by a female commentator claiming that 'The promises made on Fascist platforms and in Fascist literature are inadequate to appease the anxiety of the women folk, who naturally do not want to risk going back to where they were before the days of the suffragettes.'

> *To a genuine cynic who lived through the struggle for votes for women from 1906-1914, no spectacle is more diverting than the post-war enthusiast whose one obsession seems to be the alleged danger to enfranchised women in a Fascist Britain...* [248]

> *But what really 'gets one's goat' is the exploitation of the fight made by women such as myself, who suffered imprisonment,*

and the horrors of the hunger and thirst strike, in order to vindicate our principles in the old days of the suffragette battle... Whether the lady who is now all hot and bothered about the position of women ever took part in that struggle, or was even in sympathy with it, is not known but those of us who bore the heat and burden of that day have, at any rate, earned the right to challenge those who now want to make capital out of the sacrifices of militant women.[249]

Although Norah seems to feel that her view of the state of women's freedom is inherently correct by default of her part in the militant suffragette campaign, it does not follow that fellow former suffragettes must also be inherently correct in their view. Flora Drummond, Norah's Ulstermen campaign partner, is viciously attacked for her anti-Fascist declarations.[250] Flora Drummond was running what Norah called an 'Anti-Fascist Circus' (the Women's Guild of Empire), criticizing and calling into question the BUF, its activities and the effect this could have on women voters. The article is scathing and unrestrained, referring to her former suffragette friends as

extinct volcanoes either wandering about in the backwoods of international pacifism and decadence, or prostrating themselves before the various political parties.

[the] maiden aunts who surround her [Flora] seem to centre round the lobbies of the talking shop at Westminster, trying to persuade party politicians to do their bidding.

In response to Flora's criticism of the violent methods used by Fascism, Norah reminds her reader that Flora had once:

defied all law and order, smashed not only windows, but all the meetings of Cabinet Ministers on which she could lay hands, and was for long the daily terror of the Public Prosecutor and the despair of Bow Street!

It seems Norah could not tolerate the fact that many of her former fellow militants could not see that women's freedom required far more than a cross on a ballot paper, and that they had now been sucked into the establishment and blinded by the system. Norah remained convinced that women had not yet won freedom and could not do so through democracy. What will Flora Drummond do to solve society's problems, she seethes:

Why, simple as falling off the Eiffel Tower. The Guild is to persuade the women voters – hold your breath – to use the power of the vote!

The democratic flaw that Norah seems to alight upon time and time again, in her concern for women's lack of freedom, is in fact the lack of influence that any one individual can exert through voting alone. This is as true of women as it is of men, but Norah highlights the concern for women because she had wanted to make possible social changes to benefit women. She seems to feel that she and her friends fought so hard for the wrong thing, the thing that gave neither them, nor anyone else, any power or influence.

> *Though we shall be told that this was what we fought for, a moment's reflection will show that this [the vote] was regarded as but the symbol. Women never made the fatal error of imagining that because men voted they were necessarily free. It is the mark of the unintelligent woman today to suppose that a woman is free because she also votes, or that democracy can ever offer anything but the careful and organized exploitation of men and women who suffer it to exist.*[248]

> *...the right to put a cross upon a ballot paper once in five years, was merely a new and worse form of slavery, both for men and for women...*[249]

Norah's bitterness at the failure of the suffragettes to achieve anything for women's freedom is exercised time and again and her disappointment at her fellow suffragettes for giving up the feminist agenda is evident:

> *From those days of heroic struggle seems now a far cry. But will anyone deny that in all the long history of human effort and sublime self-sacrifice which the world has seen a greater disillusionment can be found than the complete failure of the women's movement in the post-war years? Look back, those*

of you who doubt these words, to the days when that fight was at its height; when women of sensitive nature left their sheltered homes to stand beside their working sisters, in the demand for simple justice; to keep vigil with them in the lonely prison cell; to march hand in hand through the streets in monster processions and vast demonstrations; to endure the brutality and insults of the hooligans of the gutter, and at last to come to victory and gain the victors' crown.

What high hopes then animated that wondrous band of women; what promise of high endeavour lay within our grasp? We were to bring into the new life that opened out before us all those qualities of strength and determination which we claimed to possess; we were to supply an influence with which by our very nature we were endowed. In politics we were to clean up the corruption and chicanery which we had denounced during our period of struggle under a Liberal Democratic administration; we were to bring to public life the fresh vigour of newly emancipated human beings, and above all, we were to demand and insist upon peace and the end of bloody war, in the interests of decadent governments and the vested interests that control them.

To-day not a single achievement stands to our account, and supreme tragedy faces those of us who survive, the tragedy of lost leadership, and the eclipse of all claim to have used for the betterment of humanity the unique opportunities that lay to our hands.[251]

Norah's conviction that democracy is undemocratic lies in its reliance on a Party system, and she attacks the Parties and all those who blindly follow the Party system in the search for influence. The Party system, she believed was antiquated and unfit for purpose, in parallel with Major Fuller's attack on WWI Generals. The 'Tragedy of Passchendaele' was an article published in The Blackshirt by Major General Fuller, who had fought in WW1 and which highlighted how the military strategy in WW1 had been based on traditional techniques irrelevant to a battlefield in 1914. This was blamed as much on the Generals' 'mentality and outlook' as on their inability to understand the new weapons available to them. For Norah this provided a perfect metaphor for the way politics and democracy had been working since 1914, and in her reply she draws a parallel between the Generals and the politicians of 1918 as 'being utterly incapable of understanding the new conditions that had arisen'. When women won partial suffrage, the politicians continued to operate

> ...*through the old channels just as today the political mentality of our old effete politicians is incapable of realizing that their day is done.*[252]

Norah's disillusionment with politics and the political system seems to have begun around the time she stood as an Independent in the 1918 election and failed to gain a seat:

> *What happened was that by the time women were given the vote, the democratic system was crumbling and falling into decay...Turning to various political parties, full of vigour and enthusiasm to play their part in the new world as liberated citizens, they found themselves bound and fettered by the Party Caucus and chained to the Party System.* [249]

As an old suffragette, she reveals her bitterness that none of the women who had fought as suffragettes had ever been elected to Parliament:

> *What woman is there amongst us who made that fight, who does not to-day feel disillusioned? Where are the great leaders of those days? Look through the names of the women who climbed to Parliament on the efforts of the suffragettes, and see that not one leading woman of that day has ever sat in the House. Democracy had killed them politically, and to-day they are forgotten as though they had never been.* [249]

The assertion is that women were given the vote simply to patronize and shut them up, making them think they were taking part in democratic decision making, and then shrewdly sidelining them and making them politically impotent. Women were

> *simply cogs in the Party wheels of the democratic system, marching into the lobbies at the crack of the Party Whip, helpless before the Juggernaut of the official machinery which*

> *rolls on, crushing all initiative and independence before it, and reducing every person who owes it allegiance to a mere cipher for the carrying through of its policies and its measures.*[248]
>
> *Their failure, which none can deny lies in their capitulation from the moment of their enfranchisement, to the bondage of Financial Democracy, for with very few exceptions they have once more allied themselves with the very Parties in the State which had treated them with such unprecedented contempt... they have turned again as handmaidens to the hewing of wood and drawing of water for the Party wirepullers, and they add to all this futility the cross upon the ballot paper once in every five years.*[253]

Her metaphor of male politicians as Party wirepullers who control women in politics by means of endless impotent committees producing useless resolutions is an idea well rehearsed in her writings.

While critics of Fascism complained of the notion of dictatorship, Norah makes several pertinent stabs at the false utopia of democracy:

> *Mr Chamberlin tells us how lucky we are to have freedom of speech, Press, assembly and election, which he insists are the four indispensable foundation stones of liberty. He ought to try being a National Socialist for a fortnight, and try his luck in Britain!*[254]

Norah was no doubt referring to the Public Order Act of 1936, which had banned the wearing of military style uniforms, and also required police consent for political marches. The notion that democracy is undemocratic owing to the Party whip system is not inherently an extremist one, but a legitimate area of political philosophy and debate relevant now and in the past. Nor has the debate about where to draw the line on freedom of speech provided any clear-cut answers even today. Yet Norah's answer to the flaws of democracy seems wonting. Her Fascist solutions take her away from logical argument and towards utopian rhetoric:

> *It is for this reason that such women as myself have turned to Fascism, the creed of the New Age, the Herald of all our hopes for true liberty and just freedom, of discipline and Leadership, those things which were the fundamental principles of our earlier struggle.... No woman who loves her country, her sex or her liberty, need fear the coming victory of Fascism. Rather she will find that what the suffragettes dreamt about twenty odd years ago is now becoming a possibility, and [woman] will buckle on her armour for the last phase of the greatest struggle, for the liberation of the human race, which the world has yet seen'.* [249]

> *Fascism alone will complete the work begun on their behalf by the militant women from 1906-1914. In addition it will rescue them from the vitiated atmosphere of corruption inherent in the Party system.*[255]

Norah also paints a very brief and inadequate justification for dictatorship implying no more than that it might inspire unprecedented loyalty, 'loyalty' seeming to need no further justification:

> *The Women's movement, like the Fascist movement, was conducted under strict discipline and cut across all Party allegiance; its supporters were drawn from every class and Party.... Like the fascist movement too, it chose its Leader, and once having chosen, gave to that Leader absolute authority to direct its policy and destiny, displaying a loyalty and devotion never surpassed in the history of this country...*[248]

The alternative to democracy offered by the BUF was not simply a vague utopian vision. While Norah does not set out in any detail the Fascist manifesto, she does refer fleetingly to the practical ideology underlying her Fascist state. This New Creed comes in the form of a 'Corporate State' which Norah claimed would deliver real equality and participation for all citizens. Corporatism is a system in which various groups in society (economic sectors and professional specializations)[256] are conceived as the essential parts of the state making up the whole, the organs making up the body. The House of Commons would be made up of representatives from each Corporation. There is wantonly little detail of how this would work and how this would deliver more equality to women in Norah's writing as she devotes far more of her energy to vilifying the present regime than to detailing 'the creed of the New Age, the Herald of all our hopes for true liberty and just freedom, of discipline and Leadership'.[249]

The most detailed information Norah herself gives on the Corporate State is in a spread in the Northampton and County Independent in which she is asked to respond to a reader query about the BUF position on the Monarchy.[257] Unused to writing about what the BUF is 'for', the style in this article is less colourful than usual, suggesting she may have had help from one of her colleagues more expert in this area. The details of the Corporate State under the BUF, including details about the role of women and the Domestic Corporation (which would be on equal terms with other professions), are left to Anne Brock Griggs (Chief Women's Organiser) and Raven Thompson who set out Corporatism as it would work under the BUF[256] and Norah seems not to turn her propaganda machine to these topics with much vigour. Norah was far more effective at damning that which existed than explaining that which would replace it.

Having dutifully flexed her pen on women's issues, Norah also takes up matters which are not gender specific. She attacks internationalism and collective security, promotes nationalism and empire, and occasionally reveals an underlying anti-Semitism.

In the 1930s, there was much discussion and debate on issues of interpreting the international protocols and agreements that existed for the purposes of avoiding future warfare. Europe was looking to the Hague Convention (1907), the League of Nations and the Geneva Protocol (1925) to save her from another war on the scale of WWI, and thus all border scuffles and neighbour disputes were analysed to identify the aggressor and the victim. The Covenant of the League of Nations had come out of the diplomatic ruins of WW1 as an instrument which, it was hoped, would guarantee lasting worldwide peace and prevent the outbreak of war. Norah took issue with this simplistic approach to international security, and with what she perceived to be prejudice in the labelling of aggressors. She believed that collective security was in fact guaranteed to lead to war rather than peace, and she wrote and spoke regularly on this topic including her talk to the Northampton League of Nations Youth Group[247] and her talk in Alton.[234]

Norah specifically unpicks Articles 10 and 16 of the Covenant of the League of Nations.[258] Article 10 became known as 'the Affirmative Guaranty', the effect of which was to establish 'the dangerous principle of the use of physical force against aggression' instead of the 'renunciation of force in disputes between nations'. This was supplemented by Article 16 which provided the 'machinery' for the Council of the League to define 'the nature of the armed forces to be used to protect the Covenants of the League'. Under this Treaty, Norah claimed, individual nations could be compelled to use force to fulfil its Treaty obligations and thus 'force rather than law….. would become the guiding principle in all disputes'. This was because 'the administration of legal justice was now subordinated to the will of those Powers of which it was made up'.

The outcome was that the more powerful nations of the League would dictate the course of events and would be biased in favour of their own political and diplomatic interests. Norah felt that the Abyssinian crisis illustrated her view in that the leading nations of the League, Britain chief among them, was seeking to bring Mussolini's Italy to heel through the threat of force, The Affirmative Guaranty. Norah's argument was that the British Government through the League was 'juggling' with the 'lives and destinies of the unfortunate people whom they control' and would be leading the British people to unavoidable and unnecessary war.

The Abyssinia Crisis in 1934 did expose major weaknesses in the League of Nations capacity to enforce international law and avoid war, but in rather the opposite sense to that which Norah was claiming. Although Norah was in a sense correct that Britain and France dictated many decisions made by the League and that those decisions were biased, there was never much risk of Britain going to war against Italy in 1934 and it was Britain's interest in Italy as an ally that prevented Britain using force against the Italian aggressor. In 1930, Italy had begun to encroach on its border with Abyssinia from its colonial territory of Italian Somaliland. Abyssinia protested to the League of Nations, but nothing was done. A border clash in 1934 was ignored by the League and in 1935 Mussolini launched an invasion.

Although the League of Nations failed to act to prevent this invasion, when Italy used poison gas against the Abyssinian advance, Anthony Eden in Parliament and Lord Cecil in the House of Lords attacked Mussolini for breaking with the Geneva Protocol which Italy had signed up to and which banned the use of poison gas in warfare.

In this example, Norah seems to take an entirely different argument against collective security, claiming that no treaty is binding if one is under attack. She accuses Eden and Cecil of hypocrisy in that Britain conveniently absolved itself of any undertaking under the Hague Convention not to use poison gas in WWI when they were under attack from Germany, and yet were quick to attack Mussolini when he abandoned his undertakings for the same reason:

> *The poisoned tongues of the united anti-Fascist front have nowhere been more active than in the allegations made in respect of the position of Italy and the alleged use of poison gas. Nor is the weapon of the bitter tongue confined to irresponsible nit-wits, who shout hysterical execrations at Mussolini, in season and out. For it has also been used in pompous condemnation by responsible politicians in both Houses of Parliament. The latter base their charges on the plea that Italy has broken her solemn pledge, given under her hand in the Hague Convention of 1907 and the Geneva Protocol of 1925, for the prohibition of the use of asphyxiating gases in war, and who tell us that this pledge was given unconditionally and without reservation. The exact opposite is the case. This Protocol depends for its legitimacy solely on the understanding that it was not only signed, but ratified, by the nations signatory to it, and was therefore subject to reciprocity by all.*[255]

Although the principle and logic of self-defence as an absolution from protocol seems reasonable, Norah seems to completely ignore the sequence of events in Abyssinia in which the uncontested view is that Abyssinia was being encroached upon by Italian forces and not vice versa.

This is perhaps the least logical of Norah's protestations, and such a blinkered defence of Mussolini may have helped persuade MI5 that Norah had some involvement in channelling Italian monies as discussed in the next chapter.

A further attack on collective security was in its secretive undemocratic nature:

> *Turning to the vast field of Imperial and Foreign politics, is it to be contended that the bulk of British women desire to see the disintegration of the Empire, or the orientation of the present foreign policy of the alleged National Government, whereby pacts and commitments are being made in their names and in secret with the avowed enemies of this country, while at the same time we are being left defenceless, not only for the purposes of our own immediate defence, but if the need should arise to honour those commitments? Do we indeed know to what we are being committed; what this policy of collective security involves, or what is the sinister power which dictates it?*[248]

The implication was that the League of Nations was operating without accountability to national peoples, took the defence of a nation out of the hands of the nation's citizens, and was, therefore, undemocratic. Norah's various arguments against collective security are lacking in integration, sometimes contradictory, and on the whole unconvincing, although undoubtedly the collective security arrangements in the 1930s were inadequate for very different reasons. Perhaps the struggle to find a coherent platform from which to denigrate collective security had its foundations in an unprocessed admiration for Empire building, which necessitates aggression against small nations, and which was at odds with her oft confessed affinity for peace and protection of small nations as in her campaigns in defence of Serbia and the small Balkan states to whom Britain owed friendship during and after WWI.

More consistent were Norah's ideas of nation. Norah was a confessed patriot from the moment Mrs Pankhurst demanded it in 1914. Norah's right wing swing took her into the arms of the British Empire Union and the National Party and her campaign against enemy aliens. Norah argued at that time that even naturalized Germans could not be trusted, implying that nationality was an internal unchangeable loyalty which could not be altered by time or place. This same logic applied to William Joyce who she felt should have been excused as a traitor owing to his Irish ancestry. Norah extended her position to Parliament and representation, arguing that only British subjects could be expected to serve their country in Parliament:

> *I preferred to stand as an Independent, going down with all the other women candidates on this occasion, save one. The exception was the Sinn Fein Countess Markieviecs, who though a notorious and avowed enemy of Britain, found it a perfectly simple matter under the democratic system to secure election to the Parliament of the country which she had openly boasted that she would destroy, disintegrate and discredit. She was if I remember rightly, returned unopposed. The next*

> *example was hardly more encouraging, for the first woman to be elected for an English constituency was an American born citizen, who had no credentials to represent British women in their own parliament save that she had married a British subject…*[248]

Norah's nationalism then, meant not that all non-British peoples were her enemies, but that any non-British person living or working in Britain was a potential enemy since nationality was pure and ingrained and loyalty to one's nation was a stable trait. As proposed earlier, given that Norah's parents were both born in Ireland, there is some strange discrepancy in her thinking and in her own standing for parliament, unless we conclude that Norah ignored or denied her own true nationality, or we assume that her grandmother had English parents allowing her to feel truly English.

Anti-Semitism, the most infamous plank of BUF policy, does not seem to feature greatly in Norah's propaganda. A brief and passing reference is made to the 'Jew Disraeli' as a metaphor for Conservative Party allegiance[253] which sits alongside Herbert Samuel as a metaphor for the Liberal Party and Marx for the Left. Samuels and Marx both had Jewish ancestry, suggesting she picked these two figures deliberately for her literary purpose not because of their being the best metaphors for the Liberal party and the Left, but rather for their Jewishness, thus coupling her disdain for Party politics with the permissive influence of Jews on that system.

In giving 'J'Accuse' as the title to one of her articles which sets out the failure of the Women's movement, Norah also makes implicit reference to anti-Semitism, albeit that in this case she is tapping the collective memory with a reference to an infamous miscarriage of justice against a Jew.[251] J'Accuse was the title of an article published by Emile Zola in 1898 which intended to expose the miscarriage of justice leading to the imprisonment of an innocent Jewish soldier, Dreyfus, for murder leading to a scandalous cover up by the hierarchy in the French military establishment and government. The term 'J'Accuse' had become synonymous with cover up and scandal, and no doubt Norah was seeking to align herself, in her own somewhat grandiose fashion, with the ideals espoused by Zola in his heroic efforts to save an innocent soldier with his mighty pen against the might of the French Government and Army. Given Norah's anti-Semitism, she was presumably not using the metaphor to refer to the widespread unfair treatment of Jews inherent in the Dreyfus story. While not a major plank in Norah's political edifice, anti-Semitism was undeniably part of her belief system as seen in her later life.

THE LEADER

Up until about 1934, Norah and Dudley's son Tony had been sent to a boarding school at Petworth not far from the family home. He hated school, was bullied and teased mercilessly, and was very miserable there, and while there may have been attempts to hide his illegitimacy (helped by Norah having changed her name), it nevertheless ate away at his own self esteem. Norah caused him endless embarrassment by sweeping into the school like a tornado on a whim, tearing strips off the staff for the slightest error or defect; and Tony's life would inevitably be even more miserable after any intervention Norah offered.[31]

Around 1934 when Tony was 12, he was moved from Petworth to Germany to attend school. He would boast in later life about how he had been at school in Germany in the 1930s and had joined the Hitler Youth becoming a brown shirt for a time. Having been bullied and teased at school in England, he enjoyed the feeling of solidarity offered by the Hitler Youth. He attended various demonstrations and was shown how to roll marbles under police horses' hooves to cause maximum damage, disruption and pain; and recalled Jew-baiting incidents with delight. When he was about 16 or 17, just before the war, he left school and became an apprentice pipe-fitter on the Isle of Wight, rejecting his mother's wishes for him to pursue more academic interests, given his father's status as a 'famous Oxford Don'. At around the same time (1938), with Tony no longer a burden to them, Norah and Dudley left Northchapel and moved to London. Dudley took work as a part time unpaid receptionist at BUF Headquarters, and Norah spent time working in the offices of the London & Provincial Anti-Vivisection Society.

OFFERINGS OF THE POOR

By around 1938, the BUF was beginning to struggle financially, and, through the pages of the Action magazine, Dudley proposed an appeal for funds of a most novel kind, although it can be supposed that the idea, as always, was likely to have been Norah's:

> ### *Sacrifice your Gold - How to swell British Union Funds*
>
> *In the British Union men and women have joined together in the greatest ideal this country has ever known .... It is this spirit that has prompted our members so often to make great sacrifices. It was this spirit that prompted Blackshirt Elam to give one of his dearest possessions that the Movement might survive in its struggle with the forces of materialism. He has given a gold signet ring - a gift from his mother when he was 21 - a possession to him so valuable because of its sentimental association. With his gift he has sent the suggestion that*

> *hidden away in member's drawers and cupboards may be many such valuables that could provide an untold source of wealth to the Movement...*[259]

Norah followed this gesture in an extraordinary fashion, illustrating just how little concern she had for the deceit of her false marriage:

> *'The Offerings of the Poor - Send in your Gold' – 'Mrs Elam has emulated her husband's example by sending in her gold wedding ring'.* [260]

It may have appeared to many readers as the ultimate sacrifice to the cause, to give up your wedding ring. Yet 'Mrs Elam' was not married to 'Mr Elam' and the 'wedding ring' was presumably that given to her by Charles Dacre Fox. This grand gesture served to perpetuate the myth that the Elams were married, while in private Norah was discarding a remnant of a failed relationship. No doubt the scheme was devised by Norah in an attempt to ingratiate herself and Dudley with the BUF leadership, while producing a perfect cover for her not wearing a wedding ring while supposedly being married to Dudley Elam. The Mosleys and other leaders of the BUF along with the secret services all remained unaware of the real marital status of Dudley and Norah and although MI5 became suspicious, they never managed to clarify the matter.

By now, many of Norah and Dudley's activities, along with various other BUF members, were being watched by MI5 agents working undercover. Under the gaze of the secret service, but free of the chains of parenthood and country living, Norah was able to spend more time courting the Mosleys and her London friends which included attending luncheons with Diana Mosley and Commandant Mary Allen at the Ladies' Carlton Club.[218] Mary Allen was a good friend of Norah from WSPU days and a fellow LPAVS campaigner. Norah had a large number of acquaintances, and hosted social gatherings at home impressing Mosley with her interesting guests who included Lord Cottenham, a famous racing car driver but also (unknown to Norah and Mosley) an MI5 officer. Norah remained desperate to convey the appearance of respectability and to be close to the Mosleys who were both political compatriots as well as titled socialites. Her pretend marriage, her 'royal' husband the Oxford don, and her famous and interesting friends all helped her convey the right image and to make sure she moved in the right circles. Her illegitimate son was now conveniently out of the picture.

Norah was now able to move in more illustrious BUF circles and was delighted to be in the close circle of 'The Leader'. Norah and Dudley attended the 500 strong BUF annual luncheons at the Criterion in March 1939 and March 1940[218] which were addressed by The Leader, and latterly attended by undercover MI5 agents.[261] By this time Mosley was behaving more and more like the European dictators he admired:

When the last course of the lunch was served, MOSLEY rose amid tremendous cheering to make his speech. This consisted of a bitter tirade against the Government and Jewry, and was delivered in typical 'Hitlerian' fashion. MOSLEY adopted a forward crouching posture, clenched his hands and his voice gradually increased in volume until, towards the end, he was almost shouting.'.

War was declared on 3 September 1939 by which time Mosley's speeches were full of anti-Semitic, anti-war and pro-German rhetoric. For Mosley and Norah who had both campaigned on Germanophobic principles two decades ago, this volte face is as keen as Norah and the Pankhursts' turn to patriotism in 1914, and yet would have perfect internal logic for Norah. In his March 1940 address, Mosley argued against the war:

He went on to accuse the British Government of being responsible for the war and claimed that in view of the reasonable peace terms expressed recently by Hitler, there was no justification for continuing hostilities. These terms, which were identical with the views expounded by the British Union of Fascists in 1933, before Hitler came to power in Germany, were fair and just. They still formed part of the policy of the British Union, which advocated giving Germany a free hand in Eastern Europe, and all mandated territories. In return, Germany would only be too glad to let Britain develop her Empire. He (MOSLEY) was sure of one thing; Germany did not seek world power. He had been definitely assured by Germans that this was so. Germany only wanted a chance to expand in Europe and this was her right. It was certainly not worth the criminal wastage of British lives in an attempt to stop her.

Mosley received a tremendous ovation at the end, and during the speech the audience had 'shown considerable enthusiasm throughout and cheering was loudest following his remarks about peace and the Jews'.

Norah and Dudley also regularly attended secret meetings to help organize collaboration between other 'patriotic societies'. These included The Link, The Nordic League, and The Right Club. The Right Club was a secret society that had been formed by Archibald Ramsay in 1939 to try to get unity among the different right-wing groups in Britain including the BUF. Ramsay was virulently anti-Semitic and pro-Nazi, and The Right Club included among its members William Joyce who had split with Mosley in 1937.

Many of the secret meetings, including meetings between Mosley and Ramsey, were held at the premises of LPAVS. The LPAVS had played a large part in Norah's adult life long before she had joined the BUF and the LPAVS continued to work for animal rights into the 1960s. However, MI5 and Special Branch came to suspect that it was a conduit for secret Fascist activities because of the number of leading members of the LPAVS who were also active BUF members (including Mary Allen and Sylvia Armstrong). Contrary to MI5 theories, their concern for animal welfare was completely genuine, but Norah's unconventional accounting methods may have muddied the water and attracted suspicion.

Aware that war was gathering and that internal forces were closing in on him, Mosley had begun to make preparations for eventualities such as his imprisonment or assassination. Dudley was chosen as one of eight trusted men who would take over running of the BUF in the event of Mosley being unable to do so.[262] Norah was not given this honour by Mosley, but he did ask her to 'look after' BUF funds for a short period in the event that he was assassinated or BUF headquarters were bombed. He was clearly unaware of her poor success record in accounting matters. Norah stored Mosley's money among LPAVS accounts.

On 18 December 1939, Norah's flat and her offices at the LPAVS were raided by the police where they found papers relating to Mosley's contingency plans. The list of eight names was found, incriminating Dudley. Norah was also incriminated in a letter on BUF notepaper thought to be referring to BUF funds in which Mosley had written that 'Mrs Elam had his full confidence, and was entitled to do what she thought fit in the interests of the Movement on her own responsibility'.[262] Strangely, the letter had been found inside an envelope marked 'Private and Personal Mrs Dacre Fox',[263] perhaps because within the LPAVS Norah used her former name for authorship, administrative and accounting purposes, or perhaps because as Mary Allen later revealed under questioning,

'Professor Dacre Fox' was used as a pseudonym for the Elams in the organization of secret meetings.

Following the raids in December 1939, Norah was arrested and interrogated on 23 January 1940.[263] The interrogation aimed to establish whether her handling of BUF funds had been illegal or improper. There had been some suspicion that Mosley had been receiving funds from Mussolini, and MI5 developed a theory that Norah was using the LPAVS front as a conduit for these Italian gifts. MI5 investigations had by this time uncovered her former bankruptcy, which would have made Norah an even greater object of suspicion as she would have been presumed to have experience in moving funds and hiding assets from bankruptcy administrators. Along with her dubious marital status and her past history of militancy, she began to fit a criminal bill. Her interrogators noted that 'Having regard to Mrs Elam's past experience in connection with 'Funds' I think it reasonable to suppose that she herself suggested it would be advisable for BUF money to be withdrawn from the trust account. Mrs Elam said that Mosley trusted her completely and she was proud of it.' The obvious implication is that MI5 considered it foolish of Mosley to trust a former bankrupt with party funds.

After her interrogation Norah went to see Mosley shortly before Special Branch arrived to interview Mosley themselves.

I know, he said, why you have come here today. Poor Mrs. Elam has been round to see me and has told me of the trouble she has been in. If you had only come and asked us we could have explained it all to you so easily. I simply cannot understand why you should go to all this trouble in connection with BUF finances. Our position is perfectly clear. ....As regards the money paid to Mrs Elam we have nothing to be ashamed of and nothing to conceal. When war became imminent we had to be prepared for any eventuality. There might have been an air raid, our Headquarters might have been smashed by a mob, I myself ......was expecting to be assassinated. I may tell you quite frankly that I took certain precautions. It was necessary then for us to disperse the funds in case anything should happen to Headquarters or the leaders. Mrs. Elam therefore took charge of part of our funds for a short period before and after the declaration of war. There was nothing illegal or improper about this.[264]

In fact, Special Branch had not gone to see Mosley to discuss Norah's involvement with the funds, which was a less urgent matter in spite of Norah's pride in the association it brought her; MI5 were far more interested in Mosley's knowledge of Peter Whinfield, a suspected German spy. The raid on Norah's flat and offices had in fact been in connection with Whinfield and the finds they made about BUF finances were opportunistic.

Peter Whinfield and his parents, Lieutenant-Colonel HC & Mrs Muriel Whinfield, were regular visitors and close friends of the Elams. Norah had met Muriel in her West Sussex days, when Muriel had also defected from the Conservative Party, and they had shared a platform at Alton when they were heckled and shouted down by 'Reds'. Mosley had met the Whinfields at the Elams.

During the Anschluss in 1938, Peter had travelled to Austria and had received letters from his mother, posted by Norah, arousing the suspicion of MI5.[68] Peter was known to have had contact there with Peter and Lisa Kruger, known spies. Mosley had also met Peter Kruger at the Elam's flat, and described him to the Special Branch Officers as someone who had 'written a book about the Jews, a work of scholarship' and who impressed him as 'being a serious research worker and not at all the kind of person who would act as an agent'.[264]

FIFTH COLUMN

Defence Regulation 18B of the Emergency Powers Act (1939) allowed for suspension of habeas corpus and was designed for the detention of Nazi sympathisers on the outbreak of war. In August 1939 William Joyce had been tipped off that arrests under 18B were imminent and he fled to Germany with his wife. In Spring 1940, fears that a fifth column would depose the British government and assist Hitler in taking control of Britain led to the expansion of 18B and the arrests of numerous known leaders of the far right along with suspected spies and informers.

On 23 May 1940[265] Sir Oswald Mosley was arrested as were Norah and Dudley. Dudley and Mosley were taken to Brixton Prison along with various other male detainees, while Norah was sent to Holloway with the women detainees:

Our Stalwart Women

Mrs Elam (Mrs Dacre Fox) a militant suffragette and ardent patriot was arrested with three other women, Mrs Whinfield, Mrs Brock-Griggs and Olive Hawks.[266]

Diana Mosley was soon to join the other BUF women in Holloway. Dudley and Mosley remained in contact in Brixton Prison[267] while Norah and Diana kept in touch with each other in Holloway[268].

The arrests of the Fascist leaders was widely publicised and the local inhabitants of Northchapel recognised their former neighbours in this publicity. Fear and paranoia reached comic proportions in the summer of 1940 when Northchapel locals took to thinking that the village might be being used as a centre for sending signals to German aircraft. A caravan spotted temporarily parked in the village was identified as a potential transmitter of these signals and so a number of patriotic residents set fire to it[269]. The caravan actually belonged to Captain and Mrs Manico, the BUF District Leader for Chichester, the couple having just moved to Northchapel that month.[239]

News of the arrests also reached the Isle of Wight where Tony Elam was working as an apprentice pipe-fitter. Suspicion and shame fell on Tony and he was sacked. He moved to London and stayed in his parent's flat at 5 Logan Place where he remained until the end of the war. Being the age for conscription, he went on 17 June 1941 to Acton to enlist for war service with the Royal Armoured Corps. He was ranked a Trooper and was due to go to Catterick Garrison, a large army training camp in North Yorkshire on 17 July 1941. But on 5 July 1941 the Army received a letter from GCHQ in Cheltenham working with MI5 giving an order to prevent Tony Elam reporting for duty. The day before Tony was due to travel to Catterick he went to collect his papers and was told that his 'services were no longer required'.[270]

Tony claims that he was deeply disappointed, upset and embarrassed; yet having given his address as 5 Logan Place and his next of kin as Dudley Elam, he must have known that there was a possibility of him being associated with his parent's activities. He also refused to agree to be vaccinated, which was his right (no new compulsory vaccination laws had been introduced since the mass opposition to smallpox vaccination in the late 1800s). Yet refusal to be vaccinated by soldiers and volunteers was regarded with suspicion because of its links with anti-establishment views. Moreover, there was huge pressure for conscripts to submit to vaccination, and there were various incidents of military authorities preventing conscripts finding out about the exemption[271] and stopping a soldier's leave if they refused.[272] By refusing vaccination on his recruitment form, Tony would have been giving MI5 sufficient grounds to suspect that he sympathised with his mother's views at a time when the anti-vaccination and anti-vivisection movements in the UK were still regarded as being linked with Fascism.

Meanwhile, 18B detainees were all offered the right to object to their imprisonment and make an appeal to an 18B Advisory Committee. Norah, ever the rebel, declined to appear before an 18B Advisory Committee. Mosley did appeal and during his hearing he was yet again interrogated about BUF funds. Scotland Yard were still adamant that Norah had been an intermediary for channelling money from abroad, particularly from Mussolini in Italy. Mosley was adamant, however, that BUF funds had been split up as a precautionary measure and distributed around people that could be trusted, including Norah. Mosley produced documents to show the money going in and out of BUF accounts.[273] Mosley may have been informed of Norah's bankruptcy history by his interrogators during this time, and he may have come to regret trusting her and begun to feel irritated by her effrontery.

Diana Mosley appealed against her internment and in discussions with her solicitor she sought to find ways to help the Elams whom she was clearly fond of:

Then there is Mrs Elam known as Dacre-Fox her first husband's name – she has an old husband who is not very strong, has been interned and had a very bad time at Stafford and some other prison - she is worried to death about him and also that she may have to go to the Isle Of Man it would be so dreadful for her as she can see him now and he is such a dear.
[274]

While in Holloway, Norah spent much time with Diana in her cell regaling the young women fascists with stories of her heroic times as a suffragette. One detainee Louise Irving wrote:

> *I met Mrs Elam when I was in F Wing in Holloway. I was a little in awe of her – she was of course a much older woman, and highly intelligent and erudite. Lady Mosley sometimes invited me to her cell with a few others for a small friendly get-together. All sorts of topics – art, music, literature etc were discussed, and Mrs Elam was invariably there ... I was never close enough to her to hear about her suffragette experiences, but she was certainly a staunch member of BUF.*[275]

As ever, Norah was prone to dramatics and she embellished her stories slightly, clearly making an impression on Diana and the other young women:

> *Officer Baxter recorded the following exchange between Diana Mosley and her mother, Lady Redesdale : Lady Redesdale (sic) , said she wanted to go to see the lady in Logan Place (meaning Mrs Elam) and Lady Mosley said 'Oh do, she is such a sweet dear soul and you will probably find her in the midst of a large tea – she is very fond of her food, which makes her all the more marvellous as she was here in the suffragette time and went on hunger strike three times and Mrs Pankhurst gave her a medal with three bars and she is so proud of it; the officers in those days were so different to now, they absolutely tortured those poor women – do get her to tell you all about it, it's so interesting and six of the officers*

couldn't bear it, and all resigned on the same day stating as their reason that they hadn't joined the service to torture women so they left' (I was one of the officers at that time, so I was rather amused).[276]

Whether Diana's interventions on behalf of the Elams were successful or whether the authorities felt there was insufficient evidence against them anyway, Norah and Dudley were released fairly early on in the war. Dudley was probably released late in 1940 while Norah seems to have been released by at least February 1942. They were never sent to the Isle of Man indicating that they were assessed as low risk to national security, perhaps owing to Dudley's age and ill-health, or perhaps owing to successful lobbying by Diana and her lawyers.

Although Diana was clearly fond of Norah, and in spite of Norah's efforts to portray herself as belonging to the same class as the Mosleys, her disguise was not entirely successful, and Oswald Mosley clearly began to tire of her now there was little use she could be for him. His attitude seems to have begun to change while he was in Brixton.

Mosley worked with his solicitor Mr Swan to set up a committee to work on informing MPs of the facts about detention under 18B with a view to 'aid justice' for the detainees. Mrs Dacre Fox was among the names Mosley proposed to form the committee but Mr Swan advised him that '....he did not think Mrs Dacre Fox would fit in with the other people [as] she was very domineering and not of the same class as the others so Sir Oswald agreed to cross her off the list'.²⁷⁷ Mr Swan did seem to think Norah could be useful for fundraising though, and he informed Mosley in October 1942 that '....a committee had been formed to get in money for the case (appeals to Advisory Committee) and that Mr & Mrs Elam and Miss Marsden formed the committee and he felt it was in good hands'.²⁷⁸

These initial plans made by Mosley and Swan eventually led to the formation of 18B Detainees (British Aid Fund) and the 18B Publicity Council, that were registered as a war charity under the War Charities Act in 1940. A number of those Mosley had hoped to engage such as Henry Williamson and Hugh Ross Williamson declined to be involved with the work²¹⁸ and in spite of Swan's reservations about Norah, she remained an enthusiastic and willing worker such that Mosley may have had less choice in the Council's membership than he hoped. George Dunlop ran the charity from its inception in September 1942 and Dr Margaret Vivian, Norah Elam, and Viscountess Downe were all involved in fund raising. In the course of this work Norah was described as 're-apply[ing] the tactics she had used during suffragette days when she had agitated for the release of other fellow dissidents'.²¹⁸

POLICE SWOOP— MOSLEY ARRESTED

Sir Oswald Mosley, British Union of Fascists leader.

John Beckett, former M.P., Secretary British People's Party.

Mrs. Dacre-Fox, prominent British Fascist.

A. Raven Thomson, of the British Union.

Sir Oswald Mosley, leader, and eight prominent members of the British Union of Fascists were arrested by direction of the Home Secretary yesterday. Others not connected with the Fascists were detained under Defence Regulations. These included Captain Ramsay, a Conservative M.P., and John Beckett, secretary of a Pacifist organisation. Full story on Page Two.

BUF Leaders Arrested
Front Page, Daily Sketch, 24 May 1940

PUBLICITY AND INNUENDO

When war broke out in 1939, Diana Mosley's sister Unity Mitford, who was an admirer (some say lover) of Hitler and in Germany at the time, shot herself in the head. She survived the suicide attempt and was taken to Bern in Switzerland, where she was collected by her mother and sister Deborah and taken back to England:

> *We were not prepared for what we found - the person lying in bed was desperately ill. She had lost two stone, was all huge eyes and matted hair, untouched since the bullet went through her skull. The bullet was still in her head, inoperable the doctor said.*
>
> *She could not walk, talked with difficulty and was a changed personality, like one who had had a stroke. Not only was her appearance shocking, she was a stranger, someone we did not know. We brought her back to England in an ambulance coach attached to a train. Every jolt was agony to her.*[279]

Because of Unity's illness, the authorities determined she was no threat to national security, and permitted her to live with her mother in Oxfordshire rather than imprison her as a traitor. Unity was keen to visit her sister Diana in Holloway, and Norah and Dudley offered to look after Unity at their home in Logan Place, presumably only for a short period, so that Unity could stay the night in London rather than make the journey from Oxfordshire and back in one day.

Norah was not a natural nurse and so this offer was likely to have been made to impress and gain access to the Mosleys, since Oswald Mosley had refused visits from most BUF members, only allowing relatives and 'business callers' (which presumably included his lawyers) to visit him. Norah and Dudley were almost the only BUF members who were ever given permission to visit Mosley while he was interned in Holloway Prison with Diana during 1943,[280] but it seems that this was not a mark of his regard for them, rather a mistake or even con on Norah's part.

Norah and Dudley escorted Unity to see her sister in Holloway on 18 March 1943. The prison officer present wrote of the visit:

The above named were visited this morning by Mr & Mrs Elam and Miss Unity Mitford who is staying with them at 5 Logan Place, SW.

Mr Elam talked to Sir Oswald and I could not hear what they were talking about. Lady Mosley talked to her sister first off all about Max's visit there the other afternoon while the nurse and Alexander went into Oxford to take the Guinness boys out for the afternoon to celebrate Jonathon's birthday. Miss Mitford was very delighted to have Max on his own as she hates Alexander.

Lady Mosley was most anxious to hear what they did, but Miss Mitford didn't wish to talk about that, somebody had told her that she was very beautiful but that she did not make the best of herself and she was anxious to have Lady Mosley's opinion.

Mrs Elam spoke then: she was very thrilled at getting a visit with 'The Leader'. She spoke a lot about the good work 'Darling Ann' did for the 18Bs still 'in durance vile'. She told Lady Mosley about sending her material to be made up by Mrs Raven Thomson, but having heard that she charged ridiculous prices, viz £5 for making a housecoat and £8 or £9 for making a costume, she decided to get back her material as she could not possibly afford to pay those prices.

Lady Mosley said they did seem very high prices, and Mrs Thomson would never get a connection if she were going to charge like that. They discussed the XXXXXXXX Brains Trust. Mrs Elam thought it should be called the Brainless Trust.

Sir Oswald asked them not to say they had seen him as he could not possibly see all who wished to see him and he therefore made it a rule only to see relatives and business callers. He thought it was Lady Redesdale as she had written she was coming that was why he had come along.

Mr Elam brought Lady Mosley a slab of chocolate.

Governor and Medical Officer   25.3.1943[280]

This report reveals that Mosley never gave Norah and Dudley permission to see him, and he had accompanied Diana to see her visitors because he mistakenly thought it was his mother-in-law accompanying Unity. Norah, ever the opportunist, had used her relationship with Diana Mosley and Lady Redesdale, to get a visit for herself and Dudley to see 'The Leader', and had looked after a very ill young lady in her home to secure the visit. Mosley's response must have been a disappointment to her. Norah had been keen to impress Oswald and Diana about the 18B Detainees fundraising work she had been doing, but she seems to have been brushed aside and made to feel that her visit was unwelcome.

The Mosleys were released from Holloway in November 1943 and were kept under house arrest. The 18B Detainees Fund had had a dual purpose which was to act as a cover for BUF activity and to prepare for Mosley's return to politics after the war,[218] since the BUF had officially been banned. Mosley's right hand man at this time was George Dunlop who ran the 'Fund'. With Dunlop's help he had made detailed plans for a post-war election campaign, including names of candidates who would not be readily associated in the public mind with the former discredited BUF. Mosley clearly realized that his former BUF leaders were too notorious to help him be successful and he wanted new blood to help see him into power.

The war ended in May 1945 and an election was called for July. Mosley suddenly changed his mind about taking part in the election. He held a meeting of the 18B committee on 14 June 1945[218] at his London flat and announced that

> 'recent events had .... rendered obsolete much of the painstaking work which had been prepared'. The sudden general election had 'placed them at a great disadvantage and now they must wait'. He intended to retire to the country and for twelve months would 'write books and breed cattle', but would be back 'at the appropriate time'.

Mosley's explanation for his withdrawal was general and contextual, yet George Dunlop waited until Mosley had left the room to accuse the Committee itself of being responsible for Mosley's retreat:

> It was 'thanks to some of you fellows' that the project was 'indefinitely suspended'. He had had to tolerate Flockhart, Franklin, Spicer, who all 'worked against me. The movement was killed by publicity and innuendo, and by your blah-blah's and petty jealousies, before it had a chance of survival'.

Whether or not Norah was present at this meeting, and whether any specific allegations were made about her by Mosley or Dunlop, we do not know. But Mosley's withdrawal from politics and the closing of the 18B Detainees Fund (which was effectively the former BUF), meant that Norah had no political home. Dudley was now 73 years old and had been in poor health for some years. Norah was also in her 60s. Dudley and Norah moved out of central London to live at Gothic Cottage in Twickenham. Tony, who had been living with them at Logan Place during the war moved to Southampton to start a business providing post-war construction using start-up money lent to him by Dudley. It seems that the Elams did not immediately fall out with the Mosleys as in November the secret services intercepted a birthday telegram sent to Mosley at their home in Crux Easton:

From Richmond to Mosley - Heartiest greetings and best love. Dudley and Norah Elam. [281]

By the time of this telegram however, Norah had been spending time with Arnold Leese who was an extreme anti-Semite and fascist who had opposed Mosley bitterly. Leese had an early career as a veterinarian becoming an expert in the camel. His autobiography, published in 1951, gives a clue to the two great obsessions in his life: 'Out of Step: Events in the Two Lives of an Anti-Jewish Camel Doctor'. Leese was a virulent anti-Semite, the root of which was reported to be his disgust for kashrut, which were Jewish laws laying down the correct form for preparing food and slaughtering animals. His anti-Semitism was hysterical in its intensity, as evidenced by his writings. One of his publications was called 'Jewish Ritual Murder and Human Sacrifice a Semitic Tradition', a brutal anti-Semitic diatribe. For Leese, Mosley's anti-Semitism was never adequately expressed or intense enough, and he often accused rival fascists of being soft on Jews, at one time calling Mosley a

'Kosher Fascist'. His writings and activities were such that they earned him several prison terms. In 1936 he was jailed for two articles published in the July issue of The Fascist and later was arrested under the 18B regulations. On this occasion he remained interned until December 1943, when he was released for health reasons, but later in 1947 served another six months in prison for his part in aiding members of the Waffen SS to escape.

Although heavily involved in right wing anti-Semitic movements because of the extremist nature of his beliefs, Leese was a fringe figure. After the curt and brutal dismissal of the 18B Detainees Aid Fund activists in June of 1945, Norah would have wanted new political friends. Leese shared her main lifelong concern, love of animals, also sharing her extremist right wing beliefs. It is quite possible, therefore, that she and Dudley found themselves in sympathy with Leese, and that they gravitated towards each other, finding solace in their shared experiences of now being on the fringe of fascist right wing politics. If Norah was only 'moderately' anti-Semitic during her membership of the BUF, Lesse would no doubt have encouraged the deepening of this ideology during the post-war period.

The secret services had been monitoring Leese and received information that Norah had broken from Mosley:

> *'Source SR72' - Leese (PF52953) alleged that Mrs Elam had broken away from Mosley; it was a surprise as she was a supporter of very long standing. Her reasons for doing so,*

according to Leese were Mosley's proposed conversion to Roman Catholicism and a rumour that 'Mosley will join up with Churchill in one National anti-Russian Front.[282]

There is no evidence at all to back up either of these suggestions about the reasons for Norah breaking with Mosley, and so it can be assumed that either Leese or Norah were losing the plot or that Leese knew that his listener 'SR72' was an agent and was deliberately giving misleading information. Yet the essential fact that Norah was now distanced from Mosley seemed to have some truth in it. While Norah may have lost touch with the Mosleys after their move to Ireland and then France, she seemed to have remained fond of them, particularly Diana. Norah kept a signed photograph of Diana Mosley in an esteemed place in her bedroom until she died. Of her other fascist friends, Commander Mary Allen and Arnold Leese were among the few that she kept after the war, and they are both remembered as visitors to Gothic Cottage between 1954-8. The Mosleys never visited.[31]

IF HITLER KILLED SO MANY JEWS

A MAN OF INDEPENDENT MEANS

'If Hitler killed so many Jews, why are there still so many alive?' was a remark Norah made to her son and grandchildren in the 1950s. Tony repeated this comment regularly in the 1950s and 1960s.

As the war came to a close in Europe, the German concentration camps began to be liberated by Allied troops, and photos of mass Jewish graves and reports of the discoveries of gas chambers began to be disseminated to the British public and the rest of the world. The fact of the Holocaust is in modern times an unquestionable human and moral outrage. Yet a minority of pro-Nazis like the Mosleys found the news hard to believe at first. Unlike Norah, Diana Mosley had many personal papers and interviews which provide some insight into her thinking. According to the journalist James Lee-Milne, who Diana Mosley confided in, Diana seems to have believed that Hitler could not have known what was going on in the concentration camps.[283] This was presumably her way of making sense of her own feelings towards Hitler for whom she never ceased to admit her fondness even close to her death in the 1990s. Diana also claimed never to have been anti-Semitic herself, although this is contradicted by some of her other comments and behaviour. However, unlike Norah and other members of the BUF elite, we also know that Diana was, above politics and all else, even to the end of her life, a beautiful, charming socialite who was adept at self-presentation, making her spoken political views and attitudes difficult to rely on.

Diana's failure to condemn Hitler even in the 1990s has left her in a controversial light, yet she and Oswald did at least eventually accept the facts of the Holocaust. What is now known as 'Holocaust denial' is arguably a far more serious crime. Holocaust Denial has its origins in texts such as Rassinier's 'Crossing the Line' in 1948, and 'The Holocaust Story and the Lie of Ulysses' in 1950. Rassinier made various unsupported claims denying the existence of gas chambers, and discrediting statements made by Holocaust survivors. Holocaust Denial went yet further in claiming that the myth of the Holocaust was a Zionist conspiracy to punish Germany financially after WW2.[284] Given Norah's comments about the Holocaust, and her closeness to Arnold Leese towards the end of the war, and with whom she remained in contact in the 1950s, we can speculate that she may have shared his world view on the Jewish question, which was that the Holocaust may have been attempted by the Nazis, but failed, and in this sense Hitler lost the war. In the 1950s until his death in 1956, Leese mentored Colin Jordan, a prominent neo-Nazi who was at different times a leader or leading member of the White Defence League, the National Labour Party and eventually the British National Party. Turning the Holocaust story on its head, Leese and other neo-Nazis, including AK Chesterton, argued that the Jews were responsible for the war and condemned the Nuremberg trials as:

> a 'nauseating spectacle' that failed to indict the 'sinister forces' really responsible for war. [285]

Although Norah harboured some of these views, she left the political limelight, and only pedalled her views away from public platforms to her family or to doorsteppers who got very short shrift at Gothic Cottage.

As Nazism and Fascism came to a calamitous and despicable end in Europe and Norah's ideology was smashed into disrepute, she was also facing a personal crisis. Dudley was 73 and in poor health, suffering from heart disease. Tony had left to run his construction business in Southampton. At Gothic Cottage, Norah and Dudley employed Florence Wells as a maid who was probably a cousin of Mary and Arthur Wells who had come to blows with John Doherty many years ago leading to Mary being sacked, suggesting Norah still liked to make friends of her family's enemies. Having been an active campaigner all her life, her mind was still engaged in political thinking, but Dudley's ill health required a lot of attention from her, the sort of caring for which we know she was ill suited. Their relationship had been a volatile one with frequent violent rows, in which they would chase each other round tables and furniture, brandishing objects at each other.[31] Norah clearly had little patience and few outlets for her frustration and caring for an elderly sick man would not have been a task suited to her.

Dudley never reconciled with his first family. His son Eustace did visit the UK in 1947 when Dudley's ill health and nearness to death was evident.[168] Whether or not Dudley ever had a will in which his first family were to benefit, his last will was written in January 1946 and left everything to Norah or to Tony Elam, should Norah pre-decease him. Nothing was left to Ada or her two children. The new will was witnessed by Florence Wells. In the same way that Norah seemed to have manipulated her father's affairs when he was close to and after his death, Norah no doubt encouraged or insisted on Dudley writing this will as she would have been anxious about her own financial position after his death, being unmarried. It is possible that hearing of Dudley's new will, Eustace returned to England to try and persuade Dudley to recognize his first family in his will. If so, he was not successful and in any case the Trusts that Dudley had inherited from his adoptive grandmother Carina Day seem to have all been drawn down, spent or lost in the 1930s stock market crash by this time. Dudley died of coronary thrombosis and arteriosclerosis on 3 December 1948[286] aged 76, leaving everything to Norah as sole beneficiary. Yet the Probate Certificate issued indicates that this amounted to the sum of £403 19s 9d,[287] a tiny sum compared to the £3,000 that had been set up in

Trusts in 1867 when Carina Day died. Gothic cottage was not included in the Grant of Probate and may have been mortgaged by this time or ownership transferred to Norah before Dudley's death.

Norah was left with no close family and a son of 26 with whom relations were strained. The lack of affectionate bonding between Tony and Norah was evident all his life in the way he talked about her, which was not unlike the contradictory ways that Norah related to her father. Tony was always in awe of his mother, yet never expressed any filial love or sense of duty in her earshot. Not having realised until he was nine that Nanny Pannell was not his mother (which is also when he was allowed to eat with Norah and Dudley in the dining room), Tony did not call Norah 'mother', 'mum' or even 'Norah', just 'she'. He had called his father 'Sir'.[31] Tony's self-esteem was dangerously low and Norah had a great deal of responsibility for this; including among other thing his illegitimacy, her lack of maternal love and caring, his teasing at school, dismissal from his apprenticeship and dismissal from the Royal Armoured Corps. As a young man during the war years, because of his dismissal from the Army, he may also have been suspected of being a conscientious objector, not being in uniform. During the war and afterwards, conscientious objectors were a highly despised group, and any young man of fighting age going about society during the war would have been received with suspicion and disgust, accused of being pro-Nazi cowards. Tony's experiences of life in Britain throughout his life were, therefore, all tainted with bullying, hostility and rejection which, along with his internal sense of self-hatred owing to his illegitimacy left a destructive internal force waiting to erupt.

After the war, Tony went to live and work in Southampton as a self-employed building contractor during which time he met Olive Short, the daughter of a merchant seaman. Olive was working as a cinema usherette. She was a timid, shy woman who had suffered poor health in her childhood, having been virtually orphaned at the age of five, with her mother dying of pneumonia, and her father away at sea so that she hardly ever saw him. After the death of their mother, as a result of which Olive suffered a bad bereavement reaction, Olive was sent to live with an older stepsister, Eva, and her husband. This was by way of an arrangement by Olive's father, who financed a home for Eva and her husband, on the condition that she take in Olive, her sister Beryl and brother Colin. Eva's own large family grew regularly every year, and Eva spent all her husband's earnings on cheap romance novels, cigarettes and sweets for herself. Olive was neglected by her adoptive family, and was regularly sent with the other children begging for food on account at the local shops, an ordeal that she found deeply humiliating. Olive's refusal to buy anything on credit in adult life would come to irritate Tony intensely and help to unleash his destructive core.

Olive and Tony met while lodging in a house with Mrs Tanner, a friend of Olive's father. The building contract that Tony had been working on when he met Olive had been secured by him as part of a business enterprise that he had begun with considerable start-up funds loaned to him by Dudley. The contract was for removing concrete war defences that had been constructed in a school playground. The business was doing quite well, but after Dudley died in December 1948 Norah, who was very anxious about her financial position, insisted on having the full amount of the loan returned to her immediately. Norah told Tony that the money was hers and she wanted it back, including any money earned from his present contract. Tony was unable to stand up to Norah and because this was a fledgling business, and he now had no money with which to run it, the business folded. Dudley had also owned a small library of books which included many valuable first editions that Tony believed had been meant to be left to him, but Norah sold them, arranging collection while Tony was away on a trip. Dudley's will of course, had not specified either of these agreements he may have made verbally with Tony.

Tony did, however, do much to spite his mother including working in trade jobs unworthy of his 'ancestry' and education, and marrying the daughter of a merchant seaman which Norah found highly distasteful. Norah was forced to stay with Tony and Olive at Mrs Tanner's house when she went to Southampton to attend their wedding in August 1949. Norah's domineering character led Mrs Tanner to give up her own bedroom for Norah to make her comfortable, yet Norah behaved with nothing but contempt for what she regarded as a lower class woman. At the wedding Norah made her disdain very clear along with her disgust that her son was marrying beneath him in class and intelligence, the irony being that her own incapacity to manage her finances had left her financially bereft in spite of her assumed upper-class mannerisms. When the registrar asked for the occupation of Tony's father, she said, in her 'Trafalgar Square voice', 'He did not have an occupation. He was a man of independent means'.[31]

Tony's childhood had crafted him into an aggressive bully, and he immediately followed a path of domestic violence and abuse towards his wife and children. After they married, Tony and Olive continued living with Mrs Tanner but they only had a small room with shared facilities, and once the first child, Angela, was born in 1950 it was too small. In the years after WW2 accommodation was at a premium and although the Government was building houses, ex-servicemen were given priority for housing. Tony had not served in the war, and so came low down the list for housing. The couple was forced to wait until after the Government had fulfilled what it considered its obligations to other priority groups. On leaving Mrs Tanner's home they moved on to a farm where the farmer was renting temporary caravans to people waiting for housing. The farmer then sold the land to the local Council to enable them to build more housing, forcing Tony and Olive to move again, this time to Red Lodge in Southampton. This was a large house, converted and divided up into family units that had belonged to an aristocratic family, many of whom were forced to give up their houses after the war due to the tax regimes introduced by the Labour Government that came to power in 1948. At Red Lodge Tony and Olive had a room, kitchen and shared bathroom.

In 1953 Olive and Tony had a second daughter, Christine, but by 1955 Tony was fed up with their accommodation due to the lack of privacy. The general housing shortage after WW2 continued for a long time and it was many years after the war before everyone could be re-housed. Tony and Olive, therefore, decided to move into Gothic Cottage in Twickenham with Norah. Tony obtained employment as a long distance lorry driver with Dallas Transport, transporting machinery and equipment countrywide for infrastructure projects. In 1956 Tony and Olive's third daughter, Cynthia, was born.

Living with Norah must have been a decision agreed to with much trepidation by Olive. She was terrified of Norah whom she found to be a very fearful and intimidating person, set in her views, inflexible in her demands, and who bullied her and treated her with utter contempt and cruelty. When Olive once knocked over a bottle of ink on Norah's desk and the ink spread under the photo of Diana Mosley and was soaked up, damaging a small area at bottom part of the picture, Norah flew into a terrifying rage. Until going to live with Norah, Olive had known nothing about her mother-in-law's internments or her political activities as Tony had never talked about it. Although Norah treated Olive so badly, she nevertheless spoke proudly and frequently about her past, her friends (the Pankhursts, the Mosleys), her activities and her imprisonments. She was quite evidently extremely proud of all these associations.[31] Tony was no doubt deeply ashamed given that he never spoke about any of it, even to his wife.

Tony's occupation as a long distance lorry driver necessitated him being away from Twickenham for days and weeks at a time. Norah took full advantage of his absence to victimize Olive and the children, and on several occasions she locked the kitchen so that Olive and the children could not get access to food or water. Olive would climb out of a window, walk along a roof, where there was a small drop to the ground, then climb through a window, take what she could from the kitchen and carry it up to the children bit by bit. If food needed heating, she had to carry it down the same way, and then precariously carry it back up the same route. Norah's account to Tony of this behaviour, which happened more than once, was that Olive was a liar or else she deserved it because she had 'misbehaved'. Norah's behaviour seems hardly distinguishable from the misogynist father she had spoken so bitterly about and who had driven her feminism to such extremes in her youth.

In 1958 Tony was able to move his family out of Norah's house to a home in Kingston-upon-Thames. After Norah had destroyed Tony's business in Southampton by demanding the return all of the money Dudley had lent him, he worked in many occupations, but mostly in some form of manual labour as an employee, partly to annoy Norah, who always attacked him for doing work beneath his station as a descendant of Swedish royalty, and partly to get away and stay away from his family. In those days men would be paid their wages in cash on a Friday night. Tony was by this time an established alcoholic, and took his pay packet straight to the pub on Friday nights. He spent the lot on drinks for himself and his friends, and would get home late, very drunk, with a bar of chocolate for each of his daughters, but no money left. Olive was given no money to buy food for the family and inevitably violent rows would erupt, helped along by Tony's drunkenness, during which the children cowered upstairs listening, desperately wishing it would stop.

Tony was overwhelmingly obsessed by the fact that his parents were never married. This together with the domineering, dictatorial personality style and bullying that he experienced at Norah's hands were lessons he took in and translated into a hatred of women, who he saw as weak and needing to be 'trained like dogs' to behave themselves. Tony had been bullied badly as a young adult about his status as a 'bastard' and this played on his mind. One of his favourite terms of abuse for Olive, which would be slung at her when he was drunk, was that she was a 'Whore's Bastard'. He often referred to her as a selfish nagging cow who had ruined his life. When he unleashed his furious rage and terrifying force on his family, often the only saving grace was his intoxicated state, which eventually caused him to fall over or pass out.

Sometime after Tony and his family left Gothic Cottage, Norah was moved to a home at Elmsleigh Court, very close to Gothic Cottage. She was by this time lame and could not look after herself, but was adamant she did not want to go to a hospital. Nevertheless, in early 1961 she was taken against her will to Middlesex Hospital where she died on 2 March 1961. After her death, and before Tony was aware of it, Norah's house was cleared out by an unidentified woman claiming to have been named as the beneficiary in her will. Before the cremation Tony went with his family to Gothic Cottage to find it ransacked. Tony and Olive knew who the woman was, but her identity has long been forgotten by Olive, other than that Norah was in debt to her. Later at the cremation Tony was incensed to find the ransacker audaciously present; he would have approached her but Olive, afraid of what he was capable of, persuaded him it was not the time or place. In spite of his rage, Tony never pursued a claim against Norah's estate or the mystery woman, and it is possible that Norah had accumulated so much debt owing to her trade-mark poor financial management that he felt it was not worth his while. As no probate on any will was ever applied for, or granted, it is not known what Norah's final will really contained. The cremation was brief with no speeches and no service, only the tune *Crimmond* from the hymn The Lord is my Shepherd playing in the background as the coffin slid behind the curtains.

In the frequent vicious arguments with Tony, Norah had regularly threatened to change her will and leave him nothing. In the end she did leave him nothing, but paradoxically, in spite of her struggle for women's rights and hatred of her father's bullying behaviour, Norah did seem to have ensured that Tony inherited John Doherty's tyrannical character, and the tragedy was that Tony married and had three daughters who bore the brunt of his bullying and hateful behaviour, just as Norah had endured the cruelty of John Doherty that led her to feminism. Olive and the children would frequently be treated by Tony to diatribes consisting of grossly anti-Jewish remarks, describing (with great delight) Jew-baiting incidents that he had witnessed in Germany. Norah and Dudley had instilled in their son a world view that was pro-Hitler, anti Communist, homophobic and based on a very strong and unreasonable hatred of Jewish people along with providing a very poor example of how to behave in a relationship.

In 1961 after Norah's death, Tony took his family to live in South Africa. The white South African government had, since 1948, enforced a system of apartheid in which blacks and whites lived separately. Mosley had had discussions with Oswald Pirow, an extreme right South African politician, about how to extend apartheid to the rest of Africa.[218] This obviously never came to fruition, but Mosley was undoubtedly impressed with the South African system of segregation, and Norah would have shared this admiration given that most British fascists began to extend their racist opinions from Jews to Blacks after the war. Norah's sister, Emily, had also lived in South Africa and she may have given glowing reports of life in Africa. Norah told Tony about the wonderful life he would have in South Africa where he would be able to afford black servants. From Norah's example, Tony had fully imbibed the hate filled and degrading vocabulary of anti-Semitism, which now became the basis of an extensive vocabulary to express virulent racist ideas about black people.

Left to right: Tony Elam, Olive Elam, Christine Elam
Front: Angela Elam
Southampton circa 1955

Left to right: Christine Elam, Olive Elam, Angela Elam
Twickenham circa 1956

INDEPENDENCE DAY (A PERSONAL MEMOIR)

I (Angela) travelled with my parents and two sisters by airplane to South Africa; the journey taking several days with a stop-over in Kano, where my sisters and I saw a black man for the first time. After moving around South Africa and Rhodesia in various jobs, which my father could never hold onto for very long because of his alcoholism, the family settled and were living on the copper belt in Northern Rhodesia, now Zambia, which gained independence on 24 October 1964.

When Zambia won independence and black majority rule, Southern Rhodesia (now Zimbabwe) was still ruled by a white British government, but the government run by Ian Smith was making moves towards a Unilateral Declaration of Independence (UDI) which would allow Smith to run the country without interference from London. Smith was a right wing politician who was opposed to Britain's insistence on appeasing the African nationalists, and was staunchly opposed to black majority rule. In October 1965, a month before UDI was declared, relations between the black Zambian government and its neighbour Southern Rhodesia were fraught and the Zambian Government held huge Independence Day celebrations not just to celebrate the anniversary of their victory, but to taunt their neighbours in the south. On the 24 October 1965, the anniversary of Independence Day, the whole country was celebrating.

That night a school friend, Dawn, had come to our house asking for help because she had been left on her own after her father had beaten up her mother who had been taken to hospital. My mother agreed that Dawn could stay for the night, but when my father arrived home drunk and found her there he flew into a rage, accusing Dawn of lying. Dawn's father was his friend, and he was adamant he would never have beaten up his wife, and accused all of us of being in cahoots with Dawn to spread lies about his friend. Dawn's father was called and he came and dragged his terrified daughter away.

With Dawn and her father out of the way, my father's rage intensified. With Christine and Cynthia in their bedroom, he sat on the edge of a chair in front of my mother and me. He was leaning forward with his lower arms resting on his thighs just above his knees, waving his right hand up and down while his lip quivered in rage. Venomous insults were spat at us; my mother was a 'Whore's Bastard'; she had trained me to be a prostitute; he was a 'rock in our path' who was going to stop us on our 'chosen route to infamy and hell'. At one point during his endless diatribe, I remember my mother digging me in the ribs and making a quip that I should be careful in case I stubbed my toe on the huge rock and hurt myself.

When he had worked himself up into a frothing rage and could speak no more, he drunkenly launched himself at me, thrust his hands around my neck and began trying to strangle me. My mother tried to force her small body between us, but in spite of my father's strength we managed to break away and run out of the back door, with my two little sisters who had been listening now following us. We were chased around the garden and hid behind trees until we had enough distance from him to get back into the house and retreat into the far bedroom with enough time to lock the door behind us. As we sat gathering our breath wondering what to do next, my father returned and was hacking maniacally at the door with an axe. When that failed to make progress, he went outside and attacked the window, but realising that he could not climb in quickly even if he broke it, he returned to hacking at the bedroom door. When the axe finally made some impact and we could see it coming through the door, we fled in terror, escaping through another door to the bedroom, ran through the house, out into the night and onto the streets of Luanshya, which were full of rowdy drunk young black Africans celebrating Independence Day.

We wandered the streets that night for nearly three hours, terrified of returning home. Whenever we were spotted by a group of drunken young men celebrating Independence Day, they would crowd around us menacingly and ask my mother if they could 'buy' the little girls for their wives, asking how much 'lobola' (bride price) she wanted. Lobola was normally paid in cattle, and we were told we would be cheap because we were young. Maybe they could have all three of us for one cattle. Their friends would all be jealous, they said, because they had bought a cheap white wife. We hid in ditches to escape the hordes of men on the streets. Our minds were filled with overwhelming terror and fear of the black man as our father had convinced us that black men were savages of an inferior species. We eventually risked returning home where we found my father had passed out drunk. We locked ourselves in a room together until the morning.

Sometimes, my father brought men home with him from the pub and offered them the free services of the Whore's Bastard and her prostitutes. He told them he was the master of his house and he would make his women do what he said. My mother would tell him and his 'friends' to behave or get out, and he would apologise to his friends for my mother's 'rudeness' and 'cheekiness'. Sometimes she would have to physically defend us from their advances, and the only reason she was able to overpower them with her small figure was their extreme drunkenness.

As my father gave my mother no money for food, and she refused to buy food on credit, she earned her own money doing auxiliary nursing work. She hid the money from my father to prevent him spending it on drink, and he would erupt into maniacal fits looking for the money and screaming at my mother for not giving it to him and buying the food on credit instead.

The poem 'Independence Day' was based on memories I shared with my daughter Susan, who clearly felt the anxiety and the disturbing effect of the incident many years after it happened, albeit these emotions were imparted unconsciously. I had told her no more than a basic fact about the incident; that I was chased with an axe on Zambian Independence Day; yet her teenage imagination made a multitude of emotive connections to the image and produced a frighteningly accurate account. This came as a shock and disappointment because after my own very unhappy childhood, I had not wanted to subject my children to the sort of experiences I had had. Nevertheless however hard I tried it is clear that I was unable to protect my children from my own painful lingering memories.

Independence Day

Fire crackers scream through the pestilent air
And a rotting world reeks
With terrible joy
At a senseless, brutal victory.

The night is filled with blackened fear
And a white man lurks
Behind each door
Brandishing hate on his gluttonous axe.

A little white girl wanders black streets
Dragging her sisters along.
They see the dark shadows and black silhouettes;
Not Daddy – the fuel for their darkest fear.

Amidst the cries of victory,
A childish white whimper is drowned.
And the night, it looms up and swallows her in
And she fights for her life for a thousand years.

Now I too help dig through the night
But his evil consumes us and swallows the light.
Should I let us both die in this cruel black hole
Or commit our dear daughters to captain the fight.

Susan McPherson (aged 13)

This then was Norah's legacy to her family. My father was unwanted and unloved by Norah, and made to feel that he was an intrusion and encumbrance into her and Dudley's life. When it was convenient Norah used him to further her own purposes, but eventually left him bereft in every way, both emotionally and financially. My father was unable to be empathetic, and could not make or sustain any sort of meaningful relationship, spending his life in a tortured endeavour to fit in and feel that he belonged somewhere. While not trying to excuse him for his appalling behaviour, there is little doubt that Norah never took her responsibilities to him seriously, and played a large part in shaping his personality and the adult that he eventually became. In spite of Norah's dedication to the fight for women's rights and freedom, ultimately she remains responsible for at least three further generations of women who are still wondering how to finally crush the tyrant that was John Doherty.

POSTSCRIPT

Norah's suffragette medal was sold at auction in 2006 for £7,130. We contacted the medal vendor to find out how they had come into possession of the medal, hoping to shed some light on the mystery surrounding Norah's death. Unfortunately the vendor chose to remain anonymous and told us only that she came into possession of the medal around 1969 and that she did not remember where it came from.

BIBLIOGRAPHY

1. Kean, H. "Some Problems of Constructing and Reconstructing a Suffragette's Life: Mary Richardson, suffragette, socialist and fascist", Women's History Review, 1998, 7: 4: p. 475-493
2. John Doherty. 1911 Census Household Transcript, 1911, ED1: SN276: Kew, The National Archives
3. General Register Office. "John Doherty; Mary Coombe Henwood", Certified Copy of Marriage Entry, 15/4/1868, Registrar's Office, City of Dublin
4. General Register Office. "John Doherty and Charlotte Isabel Clarke", Certified Copy of an Entry of Marriage, 28/3/1876, Parish Church of Holy Trinity, Diocese of Cork, Church of Ireland
5. O'Loughlin, Joe. "A History of Camlin Castle and the Tredennick Family", 2007, Viking Publications 0-9546605-1-X
6. Dorian, Hugh. "The Outer Edge of Ulster - A Memoir of Social Life in 19th Centure Donegal", 2001, University of Notre Dame Press 2001 0268037116
7. General Register Office. "Mary Ada Doherty", Certified Copy of Birth Registration, 3/1/1869, Donnybrook, Dublin South, County of Dublin
8. Thom, Alexander. "Thom's Irish Almanac & Official Directory", 1868, 1868-1888: Dublin
9. General Register Office. "Emily Alice Doherty", Certified Copy of Birth Registration, 5/7/1873, Donnybrook, Dublin South, County of Dublin
10. General Register Office. "Mary Coombe Doherty", Certified Copy of Registration of Death, 19/12/1874, Donnybrook, Dublin South, County of Dublin
11. General Register Office. "Francis Doherty", Certified Copy of Birth Registration, 4/12/1874, Donnybrook, Dublin South, County of Dublin

12. General Register Office. "Francis Doherty", Certified Copy of Death Registration, 14/12/1874, Donnybrook, Dublin South, County of Dublin
13. Meadley, Maureen. "Memories of Maureen Meadley of her grandfather Frank", 2010
14. Certificate of Registry of Baptism. "Charlotte Isabel Clarke", Baptism Record, 5/3/1849, Ranelagh, Dublin, Ireland
15. Church Records, Irish Genealogy Website. "Walter Clarke and Charlotte Evans", Marriage Record, 9/10/1832 Dublin, Ireland, Church Records, Irish Genealogy
16. Guinness, Henry S. "Dublin Trade Guilds", Journal of the Royal Society of Antiquaries of Ireland, 31/12/1922, Vol 12 No 2: Sixth Series: p. 143-163 www.jstor.org/stable/25513267
17. Griffiths Valuations. "Parish of St Peters Dublin (page 61)", 1858, askaboutireland www.griffiths.askaboutireland.ie
18. Irish Family History Foundation. "Norah Doherty", Baptism Record, 5/5/1878, Dublin, Ireland
19. RCB Library, Church of Ireland Dublin. "Baptism Certificates Doherty Children", Baptism Records, 24/3/2010, Dublin, Ireland
20. Hall Brendon and O'Reilly GH. "Dublin's Riviera in the mid 19th Century", 2000, Irish Genealogical Sources: 18: Dublin, Genealogical Society of Ireland
21. Paddy Rochford. "Garnavilla", Kilmacud-Stillorgan Local History Society, 28/10/2008
22. Thomas B Clarke. 1891 Census Household Transcript, 1891, RG12: 457: Kew, The National Archives
23. John Doherty. 1891 Census Household Transcript, 1891, ED11: RG12: Kew, The National Archives
24. Kee, Robert. "Ireland, A History", 1981, Book Club Associates: Norwich, Jarrold & Sons Ltd
25. Moore, George. "A Drama in Muslin", 1981, Colin Smyth, Gerrards Cross
26. Somerville, Edith Oenone and Ross, Martin. "Mount Music", 2007, Bibliobazaar
27. Becker, Bernard H. "Disturbed Ireland, Letters Written During the Winter of 1880-81", 2007, Charleston, BiblioBazaar, LLC 978-1-4264-9598-4

28. Irish Protestant Home Rule Association. "Minute Book", 28/5/1886, MS 3567: The National Library, Dublin
29. The Irish Protestant Home Rule Association. The Freeman's Journal, 23/6/1886, p. 5, Gales 19th Century Newspapers
30. Loughlin, James. "The Irish Protestant Home Rule Association and nationalist politics, 1886-1893", Irish Historical Studies, 1985, xxiv: 95: p. 341-359
31. James, Olive. "Memories of Norah Elam by her Daughter-in-law", 2008
32. Police case - Francis Arthur Wells. The Times, 14/8/1897, p. 12 London
33. Arthur F Wells. 1881 Census Household Transcript, 1881, Kew, The National Archives
34. Mr John Doherty JP Eightieth Birthday Celebrations. Surrey Comet, 9/8/1928
35. The Late Mrs Doherty, Hampton. Surrey Comet, 2/5/1924
36. Death of Mr John Doherty JP. Surrey Comet, 10/8/1929,
37. Minutes Books. "Spelthorne Petty Sessions Justices Meetings", 1922, PS/S/09/001-007: London
38. The Hamptons, The Accident to Mr John Doherty JP. Surrey Comet, 30/8/1928
39. General Register Office. "Charles Richard Dacre Fox and Norah Doherty", Certified Copy of an Entry of Marriage, 8/5/1909, The Parish Church, Hampton, Middlesex
40. John Rylands University Library, The University of Manchester. "Richard Dacre Fox, Surgeon", 24/2/2009,
41. Baby Farming in Manchester. Manchester Times, 18/3/1871, Manchester
42. Libel on a Surgeon - Heavy Damage. The Derby Mercury, 17/12/1890, Derby
43. Charles Richard Dacre Fox. 1911 Census Household Transcript, 1911, ED6: SN81: Kew, The National Archives
44. Pugh, Martin. "The March of the Women", 2002, Oxford, Oxford University Press 0199250227
45. Financiers of Militancy. Janie Allen Papers Acc 4498/6, 1914, Newspaper cuttings relating to the Suffrage movement,1909-14: Daily Graphic

46. WSPU. "Annual Reports and Accounts of the WSPU 1908 to 1913", London, The Women's Press
47. WSPU. "Annual Report and Accounts of the WSPU 1913", 28/2/1913, London, The Women's Press
48. Interview with Miss Grace Roe, Suffragette Fellowship. 23/9/1974, London, The Women's Library
49. Weekly Meetings. The Suffragette, 1/11/1912, p. 38 London, WSPU
50. At Home 4-6pm. The Suffragette, 2/12/1912, London, WSPU
51. Arrangements for Today. The Times, 5/8/1913, p. 9
52. Advert for At Home Cards. The Suffragette, 23/5/1913, London, WSPU
53. Stamper, A. "The WI and the Women's Suffrage Movement", 2007, National Federation of Women's Institutes
54. Charles Richard Dacre Fox. "Last Will and Testament", 4/7/1940, London
55. The General Secretary's Report - "Beaten All Records". The Suffragette, 14/3/1913, London, WSPU
56. Advertisement Speaker's Classes - Miss Rosa Leo. The Suffragette, 14/3/1913, London, WSPU
57. General Secretary's Report - What every Suffragette can do. The Suffragette, 25/4/1913, London, WSPU
58. Harrison, Brian. "The Act of Militancy: Violence and the Suffragettes, 1904-1918", 1982, p. 80-122 Oxford University Press
59. Richardson, Mary R. "Laugh a Defiance", 1953, G Weidenfeld & Nicholson
60. Antonia Raeburn. "Women's Hour Broadcast Interview with Grace Roe", 6/2/1968, London, BBC Suffragette Archive
61. Prisoners. The Suffragette, 7/8/1914, p. 310 London, WSPU
62. Mrs Pankhurst's Licence - The Expiry of the Period of Release. The Times, 29/4/1913, p. 10
63. Woman Suffrage – Bodyguard for Mrs Pankhurst's Return. The Times, 25/11/1913, p. 5
64. Horsewhip Prison Doctor. The New York Times, 10/6/1913, New York
65. Forcible Feeding in Prison : Libel on Doctors. The Times, 4/7/1916, p. 3

66. Miss Kenney's Health - Released Suffragist At a Meeting. The Times, 21/10/1913, p. 5
67. Miss Kenney Arrested - Violent Scene at London Pavilion. Guardian, 7/10/1913, p. 9 Manchester Guardian
68. Fulford, Roger. "Votes for Women, The Story of a Struggle", 1958, Readers Union: London, Faber and Faber
69. Militant Suffragettes Besiege Archbishop of Canterbury. The New York Times, 30/1/1914, New York
70. The Bishop of London Hoodwinked: Second Deputation to the Bishop. The Suffragette, 6/2/1914, p. 372-373 London, WSPU
71. Militants and Forcible Feeding, Bishop of London's Visit to Holloway. Morning Post, 31/1/1914, London
72. Militants Heckle Bishop. The New York Times, 2/2/1914, New York
73. Militants and Forcible Feeding, The Bishop of London in Blinkers. Morning Post, 2/2/1914, London
74. Bishop of London's Second Visit to Holloway, The Screams Explained. Morning Post, 10/2/1914, London
75. The Bishop of London in Disfavour. Morning Post, 11/2/1914, London
76. Mrs Dacre Fox's Reply to the Bishop - The Church Stands Indicted Before the Almighty. The Suffragette, 13/2/1914, p. 392 London, WSPU
77. Say Militant was Drugged. The New York Times, 17/2/1914, New York,
78. Do the Government Intend to Murder Mrs Pankhurst? The Suffragette, 20/2/1914, p. 420-421 London, WSPU
79. The Archbishop of York Interviewed on Forcible Feeding. The Suffragette, 20/2/1914, p. 421 London, WSPU
80. Appeals to the Lords Spiritual - Deputation to the Bishop of Croydon. The Suffragette, 27/2/1914, p. 438 London, WSPU
81. "Awake, Thou That Sleepest" - Deputations to the Bishops of Islington and Stepney. The Suffragette, 6/3/1914, p.462, London, WSPU
82. God Give Us Women. The Suffragette, 23/1/1914, II: 67: p. 1, London, WSPU

83. Sir Edward Carson Declares War on Women. 13/3/1914, London, WSPU
84. Sir Edward Carson Declares War on Women - Deputation from Ulster WSPU. The Suffragette, 13/3/1914, p. 496 London, WSPU
85. Militant Women Demand Equal Treatment – The Right of Free Speech. The Suffragette, 3/4/1914, p. 568 London, WSPU
86. Militants and the Police – Summonses against Mrs Drummond and Mrs Dacre Fox. The Times, 8/5/1914, p.5
87. Writ Issued Against "The Suffragette" – Mrs Dacre Fox's Contention. The Times, 12/5/1914, p. 5
88. Review of the Week - Special Notice - The Case Against Mrs Drummond and Mrs Fox. The Suffragette, 15/5/1914, p. 102 London, WSPU
89. Where is Carson's Summons? – The Government's Attack on General Flora Drummond and Mrs Dacre Fox. The Suffragette, 15/5/1914, p. 107 London, WSPU
90. Serving the Summons on Mrs Dacre Fox - Farcical Proceedings. The Suffragette, 15/5/1914, p. 107 London, WSPU
91. Militant Camps on Carson's Doorstep. The New York Times, 15/5/1914, New York
92. Pardy & Son. "London Suffragette Medal to sell at auction, Lot 354", 20/4/2006, London, www.auction-net.co.uk
93. Suffragists Sanctuary – Siege of Houses of Unionist Leaders. The Times, 15/5/1914, p. 13
94. Militants to Militants - Sanctuary Claim from Tory Inciters. The Suffragette, 22/5/1914, p. 115 London, WSPU
95. Militant Leaders Jailed. The New York Times, 16/5/1914, New York
96. Stop Press - Prisoner Release. The Suffragette, 22/5/1914, p. 110 London, WSPU
97. Cat-and-Mouse Torture - News of Mrs Dacre Fox. The Suffragette, 29/5/1914, p. 119 London, WSPU
98. Mrs Dacre Fox. The Suffragette, 5/6/1914, p. 133 London, WSPU

99. Mrs Dacre Fox Arrested – Re-Arrest of Mrs Dacre Fox – Her Appeal to the Bishop of London. The Suffragette, 10/7/1914, p. 222 London, WSPU
100. Mrs Dacre Fox Appears – Warm Reception. The Suffragette, 24/7/1914, p. 263 London, WSPU
101. Mrs Dacre Fox's Speech – No Surrender – Even unto Death". The Suffragette, 24/7/1914, p. 264 London, WSPU
102. The Price of Liberty – Mrs Dacre Fox's Third Imprisonment – Mrs Dacre Fox Re-arrested at Buckingham Palace – Mrs Pankhurst's Letter Refused. The Suffragette, 7/8/1914, p. 307 London, WSPU
103. Militants Active again. The New York Times, 28/8/1914, New York
104. Cowman, Krista. "Women of the Right Spirit. Paid Organisers of the WSPU 1904-1918", 2007, Manchester University Press 978-0719070020
105. Phillips, Melanie. "The Ascent of Woman", 2003, London, Abacus 0349116601
106. Interview with Miss Jessie Stephen. 1/7/1977, London, The Women's Library
107. Purvis, Jane. "Emmeline Pankhurst - A Biography", 2002, Routledge ISBN 0710079346, 9780710079343
108. Rosen, Andrew. "Rise Up Women. The militant campaign of the WSPU 1903-1914", 1974, p. 250 Routledge ISBN 0710079346, 9780710079343
109. Bartley, Paula. "Emmeline Pankhurst", 2002, London, Taylor & Francis Ltd 0415206510
110. Pugh, Martin. "The Pankhursts", 2001, Allen Lane The Penguin Press
111. Mrs Pankhurst Down a Coal Mine. Guardian, 28/9/1915, p. 12 Manchester, Manchester Guardian
112. Betrayal of Serbia. Brittannia, 5/11/1915,
113. Blames Sir Edward Grey. The New York Times, 14/10/1915, New York
114. The Kaiser is about to enter Constantinople. Brittannia, 19/11/1915,
115. Two Women Arrested. Brittannia, 3/11/1916

116. Liberal Press Defends Grey's Balkan Policy; Urges a curb on Northcliffe's Attacks. The New York Times, 12/10/1915, New York
117. Pathe. "Various Suffragettes Material", 1916, Pathe Newsreel
118. Enthusiasm for Venizelos. Brittannia, 3/11/1916, p. 292-cont 297
119. A Patriotic Meeting - 12/4/1916. Brittannia, 31/3/1916
120. Mrs Pankhurst at the Houses of Parliament. Guardian, 9/11/1916, p. 7 Manchester, Manchester Guardian
121. Mass Meeting in Honour of the Allied Nations - 20/12/1916. Brittannia, 17/11/1916, p. 294
122. The Women's Party. Brittannia, 2/11/1917, VI: 22:
123. Erratum. The Times, 8/7/1918, p. 6
124. Enemy Aliens – Meeting in Trafalgar Square – Demand for Immediate Internment. The Times, 15/7/1918, p. 3
125. Enemy Aliens – Movement for Immediate Internment. The Times, 6/7/1918, p. 3
126. A Clean Sweep - Poster re Demonstration Albert Hall. 5/11/1918, London, Imperial War Museum
127. Prime Minister and Aliens - Task of Committees - Concern in the Country. The Times, 20/7/1918, p. 3
128. Enemy Aliens - Strong Public Feeling - Messages from Important Centres. The Times, 19/7/1918, p. 3
129. Enemy Aliens - Demand for a "Clean Sweep.". The Times, 26/7/1918, p. 3
130. Outside the Gates - The Enemy Alien Danger. The British Journal of Nursing, 27/7/1918, 61: p. 70
131. Arrangements for Today - City Men's Meeting. The Times, 16/8/1918, p. 9
132. German Influence - Master Bakers' Demand for Drastic Measures. The Times, 29/8/1918, p. 3
133. Enemy Aliens - Sankey Committee at Work - Public Meeting in the Country. The Times, 14/8/1918, p. 3
134. Enemy Aliens – Protest in Hyde Park. The Times, 22/7/1918, p. 3
135. German Influence - Petition with 1,250,000 Signatures. The Times, 26/8/1918, p. 3

136. Riotous Scenes at a London Meeting. Guardian, 2/9/1918, p. 8 Manchester, Manchester Guardian
137. Armistice A Soldier's Question. The Times, 4/11/1918, p.3
138. Spink. "London Suffragette Medal to sell at auction", 20/4/2006, London, www.spink.com
139. The General Election: first list of candidates. The Times, 26/11/1918, p. 4
140. Defries, Harry. "Conservative Party Attitudes to Jews, 1900-1950", 2001, Southgate, Taylor & Francis Ltd
141. Arrangement for Today. The Times, 17/2/1919, p. 13
142. The "German Garrison" in Britain. The Times, 20/3/1919, p 7
143. German Variety Artists - The Protest Against their Importation. The Times, 19/3/1920, p. 14
144. Sir Alfred Mond's Libel Actions - The Swansea Election of Last Year. The Times, 8/11/1919, p. 14
145. Letter written to the Editor of the Times. The Times, 10/4/1920, p. 7
146. The Child of the Unmarried Mother. The Suffragette, 4/6/1915, p. 264 London, WSPU
147. Newsletter of the Suffragette Fellowship 1951-1977. 1977, London, The Women's Library
148. General Register Office. "Carina Descou and William Frederick Elam", Certified Copy of an Entry of Marriage, 22/4/1868, St Nicholas Church, Parish of Brighton,
149. England & Wales Marriages 1538-1940. "Ann Vallance and Thomas William Elam", 2010, ancesrtry.co.uk
150. General Register Office. "Carina Mary S De Valence Elam and Walter Frederick William Wheatley", Certified Copy of an Entry of Marriage, 22/9/1923, Roman Catholic Chapel, Vineyard, Richmond, Surrey
151. Etat Civil Belgique. "Julie Josephine Neeteson", Certified Copy of an Entry of Birth, 20/10/1818, Ghent, Belgium
152. Boyce, S. "Descou Ancestry", 2009
153. Etat Civil Belgique. "Petrus Overall Julianus Descou", Certified Copy of an Entry of Birth, 9/5/1848, Ghent, Belgium
154. General Register Office. "Petrus Overall Julian Descou", Certified Copy of and Entry of Death, 14/8/1856, Wadhurst, County of Sussex

155. Arthur Descou. 1861 Census Household Transcript, 1861, RG9: 512: Kew, The National Archives
156. General Register Office. "Arthur Julian Descou", Certified Copy of and Entry of Death, 20/9/1864, Salehurst, Ticehurst, County of Sussex
157. Carina Day. "Last Will and Testament", 26/2/1846, Brighton
158. General Register Office. "Julie Josephine Bernardine Descou", Certified Copy of and Entry of Death, 24/10/1902, Worthing, East Preston
159. Selinko, Annemarie. "Desiree", 1953, Bender & Dickes translation: Phoenix Press London 1-84212-521-4
160. Oxford University. "Keeble College Centenary Register", 1893, KC/MEM 2 A2/12 - A7/1: Oxford
161. Church of England. "The Parish of St Augustine of Canterbury, Highate, London", 10/5/2009, London, www.SaintAugustine.org.uk
162. Amato, J. A. "Rethinking home: a case for local history", 2002, CA, University Presses of California, Columbia and Princeton 0520232933
163. Edward Dudley Elam. 1911 Census Household Transcript, 1911, ED23: SN5: Kew, The National Archives
164. General Register Office. "Evelyn Anthony Christopher Fox", Certified Copy of an Entry of Birth, 29/5/1922, Kensington South, County of London
165. The London Gazette, 23/11/1928, p. 7737
166. UK Outgoing Passenger Lists. 1922, PM21: Page 8: P&O Steamship Line
167. P&O Steam Navigation Company. "UK Incoming Passenger Lists, 1878-1960", 1930, BT26: 936:
168. Union Castle Mail Steamship Company Ltd. "UK Incoming Passenger Lists, 1978-1960", 1947, BT26: 1231:
169. General Register Office. "Ada Matilda Elam", Certified Copy of and Entry of Death, 2/3/1962, Richmond, Surrey
170. General Register Office. "Sands, Mary Ada", Certified copy of an entry of death, 27/2/1893, Greenlands, Fairfax Road, Teddington, General Register Office

171. General Register Office. "Pinto-Leite, Augustus", Certified copy of an entry of death, 24/12/1958, Folkestone, Kent, General Register Office
172. Emily Pinto-Leite. UK Incoming Passenger Lists, 1878-1960, 9/3/1919, Microfilm Class B26 659: 167: Kew, The National Archives
173. Kean, Hilda. "Animal Rights; political and social change in Britain since 1800", 2000, p. 181 Reaktion Books 1861890613
174. RSPCA Meeting Disturbance - Summons for Alleged Assault. The Times, 17/7/1931, p. 11 London
175. Sir Robert Gower Summoned - Scene at RSPCA Meeting. Guardian, 12/7/1931, Manchester, Manchester Guardian
176. Protest Against Dog Film. Guardian, 2/3/1932, p. 4 Manchester, Manchester Guardian
177. Anti-Vivisectionists' "Civil War". Guardian, 20/2/1935, p. 6 Manchester, Manchester Guardian
178. Chimpanzees' Nurse. Guardian, 25/2/1946, p. 4 Manchester, Manchester Guardian
179. DA Pinto-Leite and Director & Staff. "Correspondence between D Pinto-Leite and Zoological Society of London", 1957, London
180. Table Talk by Pendennis. Guardian, 8/12/1957, p. 16 Manchester, Manchester Guardian
181. Teutonic: Francis Doherty. New York Passenger Lists, 1820-1957, 23/2/1909, Microfilm Serial 15, T715_103: 247: Kew, The National Archives
182. GRO New South Wales. "Redmond Doherty", Certified Copy of and Entry of Death, 5/6/1940, State Hospital Municipality of Liverpool, Sydney, New South Wales
183. Adriatic: Hugh Doherty. New York Passenger Lists, 1820-1957, 7/7/1911, Kew, The National Archives
184. Fifteenth Census of the United States. 1930, ED 41-46: Supervisor's District 7, Sheet 5A
185. US Army Registration Card. 1913, Serial Number 4412: Draft Number 1090

186. Records of the Supreme Court, Family Division. "Divorce Court file re Divorce Petition of Violet Austin Doherty", 8/4/1927, Reference J 77/2396/4876: London, The National Archives, Kew
187. General Register Office. "John Doherty Jnr", Certified Copy of and Entry of Death, 1/1/1930, 68 Palewell Park, Mortlake, Richmond
188. Army Service Corps. "Neal Gerald Doherty", Short Service Commission, 26/5/1916, Army Form B2503
189. Case No 1109 of 1926. "Issue of Bankruptcy Notice, Neal Gerald Doherty", London Gazette, 10/9/1926, p. 5948 London, TSO (HM Stationery Office)
190. Case No 1109 of 1926. "Bankruptcy Release Order, Neal Gerald Doherty", London Gazette, 24/4/1928, p. 2960 London, TSO (HM Stationery Office)
191. Case No 16 of 1928. "Bankruptcy Order, Dorothy Louisa Doherty", London Gazette, 8/1/1928, p. 1019 London, TSO (HM Stationery Office)
192. Case No 16 of 1928. "Bankruptcy Release Order, Dorothy Louisa Doherty", London Gazette, 22/4/1932, p. 2702 London, TSO (HM Stationery Office)
193. Cunard: Frank Doherty. UK Incoming Passenger Lists, 1878-1960, 25/11/1929, Kew, The National Archives
194. In Memoriam, Charlotte Doherty. The Times, 4/5/1929, Royal Edition: 45,194: p. 4
195. General Register Office. "John Doherty", Certified Copy of and Entry of Death, 6/8/1929, Kingston, Hampton, Middlesex
196. Funerals - Mr J Doherty. The Times, 10/8/1929, p. 13
197. Estate Administration. "Intestacy Certificate of John Doherty", 1929
198. Legal Notices - John Doherty Estate. The Times, 31/8/1929, p4
199. George Hedley Vicars Bulyea, Lieutenant Governor Canada. "Appointment of Commissioner of Oaths Canada for Frank Doherty", 1912, Government House, Edmonton, Alberta Canada, Government of Canada

200. First Meetings and Public Examinations: ELAM, Norah. London Gazette, 8/9/1931, p. 5883 London, TSO (HM Stationery Office)
201. Applications for Discharge: ELAM, Norah. London Gazette, 21/2/1933, p. 1240 London, TSO (HM Stationery Office)
202. Discharge Notices: ELAM, Norah. London Gazette, 11/4/1933, p. 5883 London, TSO (HM Stationery Office)
203. Stable, Wintringham Norton. "The Bankruptcy Law and Practice of England", Journal of the National Association of Referees in Bankruptcy, 1931, 1931-1932: January: p. 82-85
204. London and Provincial Anti-Vivisection Society. "57th Annual Report", 31/3/1933, London, The Carlton Press, Broadway, Chesham, Available The British Library Shelfmark AR 198
205. London and Provincial Anti-Vivisection Society. "62nd Annual Report", 31/3/1938, London, The Carlton Press, Broadway, Chesham, Available The British Library Shelfmark AR 198
206. London and Provincial Anti-Vivisection Society. "59th Annual Report", 31/3/1935, London, The Carlton Press, Broadway, Chesham, Available The British Library Shelfmark AR 198
207. Durbach, Nadja. "Bodily Matters - The Anti-Vaccination Movement in England 1983-1907", 2005, North Carolina, Duke University Press
208. French, Richard D. "Antivivisection and Medical Science in Victorian Society - Act of 1876", 1975, Princeton University Press
209. Hardy, Ann. ""Straight Back to Barbarism"; Antityphoid Inoculation and the Great War, 1914", Bulletin of the History of Medicine, 2010, 74: 2 (2000): p. 265-290
210. Magazine Data File. "The Animals' Guardian", Magazine Data File, 2009, www.philsp.com/data/data019.html
211. Dog's Bill. The Times, 16/3/1921, p. 2
212. Women and the Dog's Bill - Anti-Vivisectionist's Appeal. The Times, 17/3/1921, p. 9
213. Medical Research Committee. "Third Annual Report ", 1917, Cd 8825: p. 37 London, Her Majesty's Stationery Office
214. Medical Research Committee. "Fourth Annual Report ", 1917, Cd 8981: p. 25 London, Her Majesty's Stationery Office

215. Fox, Norah Dacre. "The Vitamin Survey, A Reply", 1934, London, The London & Provincial Anti-Vivisection Society, The British Library Shelf Mark 7383.e.38
216. Fox, Norah Dacre. "The Medical Research Council, What it is and How it Works", 1935, London, The London & Provincial Anti-Vivisection Society, The British Library Shelf Mark D-07680.bb.32
217. West Sussex Conservative Association. "General Purposes & Finance Committee", West Sussex Records Office Additional Manuscripts, 1945, Minute Books (May 1924 - December 1945): 12,087 - 12,088: Chichester
218. Dorril, Stephen. "Blackshirt, Sir Oswald Mosley and British Fascism", 2006, London, Penguin 9780670869992
219. Conservative Leader Resigns - Futile Policy of the Tories. The Fascist Week, 30/3/1934, p. 8 Fascist Week Ltd
220. Crowded Meeting at Chichester. Blackshirt, 4/5/1934, p. 4 Blackshirt Ltd
221. Martland, Peter. "Lord Haw Haw - The English Voice of Nazi Germany", 2003, The National Archives 1 903365 17 1
222. Official Gazette and Bulletin - Provincial Promotions. Blackshirt, 11/5/1934, p. 4, Blackshirt Ltd
223. Lady Mosley Presents Purse to Duchess of York. Blackshirt, 11/5/1934, p. 2, Blackshirt Ltd
224. British Union. "Rules of Organisation", Records created or inherited by the Home Office, Ministry of Home Security, and related bodies, 3/1938, HO 144/21281: Kew, The National Archives
225. Blackshirt Camp Opened. Blackshirt, 10/7/1934, p. 11 Blackshirt Ltd
226. Successful Meeting at Littlehampton. Blackshirt, 17/8/1934, p. 2 Blackshirt Ltd
227. Concluding Stage of Worthing Proceedings - Charge of Riotous Assembly. Blackshirt, 23/11/1934, p. 4 Blackshirt Ltd
228. Blackshirt News: Extracts from Local Reports (Midhurst). Blackshirt, 20/12/1935, p. RS139 Blackshirt Ltd
229. Financiers Waiting to Fleece India. Blackshirt, 18/1/1935, p. 18 Blackshirt Ltd

230. Our Reader's Views - Dangers of Meddling. Blackshirt, 6/9/1935, p. 7 Blackshirt Ltd
231. Correspondence - Congratulations. Action, 19/3/1936, p. 8 Fascist Press
232. Activities at Basingstoke. Blackshirt, 1/2/1935, p 6 Blackshirt Ltd
233. Blackshirt News: Extracts from Local Reports (Bognor Regis). Blackshirt, 13/9/1935, p. RS125 Blackshirt Ltd
234. Blackshirt News: Extracts from Local Reports (Alton). Blackshirt, 20/9/1935, p. RS126 Blackshirt Ltd
235. On the March - Portsmouth and Southsea. Blackshirt, 25/7/1936, p. 6 Blackshirt Ltd
236. Reds Deny Women Speakers Free Speech. Action, 7/11/1936, 38: p. 5 Fascist Press
237. On the March - Report from Guildford. Blackshirt, 13/2/1937, p. 6 Blackshirt Ltd
238. First Time she will not use her Vote. Blackshirt, 8/11/1935, p. 6 Blackshirt Ltd
239. Booker, J. A. "Blackshirts on Sea", 1999, London, Brockingday Publications 09515253 1 X
240. Legions on the March - Chichester (North Chapel). Blackshirt, 27/11/1937, p. 6 Blackshirt Ltd
241. Fascist Candidates for Parliament – First List of Twelve. The Times, 19/11/1936, p. 9
242. Prospective British Union Parliamentary Candidates. Action, 21/11/1936, 40: p. 7 Fascist Press
243. Birthday Honours for Distinguished Service. Blackshirt, 2/10/1937, p. 7 Blackshirt Ltd
244. Elam, Norah. "Why I Am Contesting Northampton", Northampton and County Independent, 27/11/1936, p. 14 Northampton
245. Coupland, Philip M. "The Blackshirts in Northampton, 1933-1940: a postscript", 2009, http://www.philipcoupland.com/the-blackshirts-in-northampton---postscript.php
246. Northampton Meets Prospective British Union Candidate. Action, 28/11/1936, 41: p. 7 Fascist Press

247. Fascists and the League. Northampton and County Independent, 1937
248. Elam, Norah. "Fascism, Women and Democracy", Fascist Quarterly, 1935, 1: p. 290-298
249. Fascism will Mean Real Equality. Blackshirt, 22/2/1935, p. 2 Blackshirt Ltd
250. Elam, Norah. "Suffragette in Anti-Fascist Circus - Flora Drummond Tries Bluffing the Women", Blackshirt, 25/9/1937, p. 8 Blackshirt Ltd
251. Elam, Norah. "J'Accuse: Failure of Women's Movements", Action, 8/10/1938, p. 14 Fascist Press
252. Tragedy of Passchendale. Blackshirt, 23/11/1934, p. 12 Blackshirt Ltd
253. Elam, Norah. "Women and the Vote", Action, 26/3/1936, p. 8 Fascist Press
254. Specially Reviewed by Norah Elam. "A False Utopia by William Henry Chamberlin", Action, 25/9/1937, 84: p. 16 Fascist Press
255. Elam, Norah. "A Great Illusion - Poisoned Gas and Poisoned Tongues", Action, 21/5/1935, p. 8 Fascist Press
256. Gottlieb, Julie V. "Feminine Fascism - Women in Britain's Fascist Movement", 2003, London, IB Tauris & Co Ltd 1860649181
257. Elam, Norah. "How do the Fascists Regard the Monarchy?", Northampton and County Independent, 15/1/1937, Northampton
258. Elam, Norah. "The Affirmative Guaranty", Fascist Quarterly, 1/1/1936, p. 101-107
259. Sacrifice Your Gold - How to Swell British Union Funds. Action, 16/4/1938, 113: p. 7 Fascist Press
260. The Offerings of the Poor - Send in Your Gold. Action, 7/5/1938, 116: p. 8 Fascist Press
261. Metropolitan Police. "Report re Criterion Annual Luncheon British Union", Records created or inherited by the Home Office, Ministry of Home Security, and related bodies, 5/3/1940, HO 45/24895: Kew, The National Archives

262. Letter from Mosley passing authority. Records created or inherited by the Home Office, Ministry of Home Security, and related bodies, 5/8/1940, HO 283/48: Kew, The National Archives
263. Cross Reference - Sir Oswald Mosley - 23/1/1940. 1940, KV2/884: Microform Academic Publishers
264. Visit to British Union Headquarters in Gt Smith Street - 24/1/1940. 1940, KV2/884: p. 1-4 Microform Academic Publishers
265. Leading Fascists Arrested – Sir O Mosley and Eight Others – MP Detained. The Times, 24/5/1940, p. 6
266. Our Stalwart Women. Action, 6/6/1940, 222: p. 1 Fascist Press
267. Governor and Medical Officer Holloway. "Copy letter Brixton Prison Governor", 1940, KV2 884: Kew, National Archives
268. Letter to Captain Clayton - June 1940. 1940, KV2/884: Microform Academic Publishers
269. Bruce, Pamela. "Northchapel, A Parish History", 2000, Northchapel Parish Council 0 9538291 0 3
270. Royal Armoured Corps. "Evelyn Anthony Christopher Elam", Territorial Army, 17/6/1941, Army Form E531/B200B
271. Vaccination and Inoculation. HANSARD: HC Deb, 2/7/1940, 362: c649: UK Parliament
272. Vaccination and Inoculation. HANSARD: HC Deb, 25/2/1941, 369: c345: UK Parliament
273. Interview with Oswald Mosley. Records created or inherited by the Home Office, Ministry of Home Security, and related bodies, 2/7/1940, HO 283/13 & KV2/885: p. 76-79 Kew, The National Archives
274. Holloway Prison Guard. "Solicitor visit to Diana Mosley", 1941, KV/1364: p. 78 Microform Academic Publishers
275. Eustance, C, Ryan J, and Ugolini L. "A Suffrage Reader", 2000, Continuum International Publishing Group, 2000 0718501780, 9780718501785
276. Torres, Governor & Medical Officer Holloway. "Report of visit to Lady Mosley by Lady Redesdale", Records created or inherited by the Home Office, Ministry of Home Security, and related bodies, 9/2/1942, HO 45/24891: p. 444 Kew, The National Archives

277. The Governor, Holloway Prison. "No 1 Sir O Mosley 18B", 1942, KV/886: p. 78 Microform Academic Publishers
278. G2 Division and Governor Holloway Prison. "No1 Sir Oswald Mosley 18B", Records created or inherited by the Home Office, Ministry of Home Security, and related bodies, 1942, HO 45/24891: p. 383 Kew, The National Archives
279. Mitford, Deborah. "Letter: My Sister and Hitler - Unity Mitford's War", The Observer, 8/12/2002, London,
280. The Governor, Holloway Prison. "Sir Oswald & Lady Mosley 18Bs", 18/3/1943, KV/887 & H45/24891/342: p. 84 Microform Academic Publishers
281. Telephone Check on Ramsbury 242 - Mosley. 1945, KV2/890: Microform Academic Publishers
282. Section B1C. "Extract - Mosley", 1945, KV/890: Microform Academic Publishers
283. Lees-Milne, James. "Obituary: Diana Mosley", The Independent, 13/8/2003, London
284. Austin, B. S. "A Brief History of Holocaust Denial", Jewish Virtual Library, 2009, www.jewishvirtuallibrary.org/jsource/Holocaust/denialbrief.html
285. Macklin, G. "Very Deeply Dyed in Black: Sir Oswald Mosley and the Postwar Reconstruction of British Fascism ", 2007, I B Tauris & Co Ltd 1845112849
286. General Register Office. "Edward Descou Dudley Vallance Elam", Certified Copy of and Entry of Death, 3/12/1948, Twickenham, Middlesex
287. Will and Probate Certificate. 1948, Principal Probate Registry

INDEX

Abyssinia Crisis 1934, *190–91*
Act of Union, 1800, *14*
Administration of Estates Act, 1925, *134*
Advisory Committee 18B, *209, 212*
Allen, Mary, *4, 150, 200, 202, 203, 221*
Anti-Alien, *95, 98, 106*
Anti-Semitism, *188, 194, 195, 219, 235*
Anti-Vaccination, *141, 142, 144, 146*
Anti-vivisection, *128, 139, 142, 150, 208*
Astor, Lady Nancy, *87, 142, 146, 156*
Astor, Viscount Waldorf, *146*
Ballyshannon, *7–9*
Bankruptcy, *136–37*
Bayly, Dr Beddow, *145*
Bernadotte, General Jean Baptiste, *2, 116*
Bernadotte, Oscar, *116–17*
Besant, Annie, *142, 171*
Bevan, Aneurin, *155*
Black and Tans, *155–61*
Blackshirt Summer Camp, *163*
Blackshirt, The, *164, 168, 170, 177, 183*
Bonaparte, Napoleon, *116*
Bradlaugh, Charles, *171, 172*
Britannia, *89–93*
British Empire Union, *95, 97, 100, 101, 106, 193*
British National Party, *225*
British National Socialist League, *160*
British Union of Fascists, *4, 150, 155, 163, 169, 172, 198, 201*
Brixton Prison, *206, 211*
Buckingham Palace, *77*
Carlton Club, Ladies, *200*
Carson, Sir Edward, *56, 59, 61, 63, 66, 69, 71, 77, 108*
Cat & Mouse Act, *40, 44–47, 76, 77, 78*

Church of England-
    Archbishop of Canterbury, *47, 48, 51, 54*
    Archbishop of York, *55*
    Bishop of London, *47*
    Bishop of Winchester, *47*
    Bishops of York, Croydon, Lewes, Islington & Stepney, *47, 55*
Church of Ireland, *10, 14, 18*
Clary, Desiree, *116*
Clary, Julie, *116*
Collective Security, *172, 178, 188, 189, 191, 192*
Compulsory Vaccination Act 1853, *140*
Corporate State, The, *187–88*
Cottenham, Lord, *200*
Dacre Fox, Charles, *25, 33, 111*
Dacre Fox, Norah. *See* Elam, Norah
Dacre Fox, Richard, *25–26*
Davison, Emily Wilding, *40*
Detainees Aid Fund, 18B, *212, 217, 218, 220*
Dog's Bill, The, *145*
Doherty, Charlotte, *10, 11, 133*
Doherty, John, *7, 9, 22, 23, 96, 133*
Drummond, Captain George, *170*
Drummond, General Flora, *61, 64, 66, 69, 88, 177*
Dunlop, George, *217*
Elam, Dudley
    18B detention 1939, *206*
    Birth, *114*
    BUF - Bronze Award, *169*
    Conservative Party activities 1922-1934, *153–54*
    Conservative Party resignation 1934, *157–58*
    Death, *226*
Elam, Norah
    Bankruptcy 1931-1933, *136–37*
    Birth, *12*

BUF - 18B Detainees Aid Fund activities, *211–12*
BUF - Fascism Next Time campaign, *167*
BUF - Handling of funds, *203–6*
BUF - West Sussex activities, *153–70*
BUF Northampton Election Campaign, 168–72
BUF secret meetings, *202–4*
Death, *233*
Detention 18B 1939, *206–11*
Detentions - Cat & Mouse 1914, *72–79*
Diana Mosley, relationship with, *209–11*
Holloway Visit with Unity Mitford, *214–17*
Independent Candidate 1918 Election, *105–9*
Setting up home with Dudley Elam, *111*
WSPU - Carson Campaign, *59–69*
WSPU Church Campaign re Cat & Mouse Act, *47–56*
WSPU General Secretary, *34*
WSPU Kingston Division, 31
WSPU Relationship with Christabel Pankhurst, *35*
Elam, Tony, *1, 120, 207, 226*
Emergency Powers Act, Defence Regulation 18B, *206*
Fascist Quarterly, *177*
Fifth Reform Bill 1928, *104*
Fordyce, Dr Dingwall, *112*
Fox, Evelyn Anthony Christopher. *See* Elam, Tony
Garnavilla, *12, 13, 20*
Geneva Protocol 1925, *188*
George, Lloyd, Prime Minister, *97, 146*
Gladstone, William, 59
Grey, Sir Edward - Forteign Minister, *91*
Hague Convention, The (1907), *188–91*
Hitler Youth, *197*

Hitler, Adolf, *109, 155, 156, 214, 223, 224*
Holloway Prison, *46, 79, 207, 214*
Holocaust, *225*
Home Rule Bills, *59, 60*
India Bill 1935, *164*
Irish Nationalism, *15, 60*
Irish Protestant Home Rule Association, *16*
Irish Republican Army, *159*
Irish Republican Brotherhood, *159*
Jenkins, JG, Premier South Australia, *100*
Joyce, William, *160, 161, 163, 168, 202, 206*
Kenney, Annie, *29, 40, 45, 46, 76, 88, 94*
Kipling, Rudyard, *95*
Lansdowne, Lord, 5th Marquis, *67*
Lauder, Harry, *95*
League of Nations, *172, 188*
Leese, Arnold, *219–20*
Liberal Prime Ministers
    Asquith, Herbert, *24*
    Bannerman, Henry Campbell, *24*
    Lloyd George, David, *24*
Link, The, *202*
London & Provincial Anti-Vivisection Society, *5, 139, 170, 198*
Lord Haw Haw. *See* Joyce, William
Lusitania, *94*
Lytton, Lady Constance, *47*
MacDonald, Ramsey, *101*
Markievics, Constance, *16*
Married Women's Property Act 1882, *134*
Maxse, Leo, *100*
McKenna, Home Secretary, *44, 71, 73, 78*
Medical Research Council, *93, 145–48*
Mitford, Unity, *157, 214, 215, 217*
Mosley, Diana. *See* Elam, Norah - Relationship with
Mosley, Sir Oswald
    18B detention 1939, *206*

Annual Criterion lunches, *200–202*
Early political career 1918-1931, *154–55*
Founding of BUF, *155*
Northampton Election campaign visit with Norah, *170*
Plans for 18B Detainees Aid Fund and Publicity, *211–12*
Roles given to Elams in event of war, *203–4*
Use of Norah's propaganda talents, *177*
Withdrawal from 1945 Election, *217*
Worthing arrest, *163*
Mussolini, Benito, *190–92, 204, 209*
National Insurance Act 1913, *146*
National Party, The, *95, 97, 100, 105, 193*
Nordic League, The, *202*
Old Forge, The, *124*
Olympia Rally 1934, *162, 163*
Page Croft, General & MP, *100*
Pankhurst, Christabel, *34, 39*
Pankhurst, Emmeline, *29, 78, 91, 113*
Parliament (Qualification of Women) Act 1918, 105
Parnell, Charles Stuart, *15, 59*
Penal Times, The, *14*
Pirow, Oswald, *235*

Prisoners Temporary Discharge for Ill Health Act 1913. *See* Cat & Mouse Act
Public Order Act 1936, *162, 186*
Ramsay, Archibald, *202*
Redesdale, Lady, *142, 210, 217*
Representation of the People Bill 1917, *104*
Richardson, Mary, *4, 39, 78*
Right Club, The, *202*
Roe, Grace, *40, 87, 113*
Rumanian Crisis, *90–93*
Selinko, Annemarie, *118*
Serbia. *See* Rumanian Crisis
Stephen, Jessie, *85–86, 113*
Suffragette Fellowship, The, *113*
The Good Body, *142*
Ulster Unionist Party, *59*
Unrestricted Submarine Warfare, *94*
Vaccination Act 1907, *141*
Van Coppenole, Dr Francois Bernard, *117*
Variety Artists' Federation, *106*
Versailles, Treaty of, *108, 109*
War Charities Act 1940, *212*
West Sussex Conservative Association, *153*
Women's Freedom League, *94*
Women's Victory Celebration, 104
Wright, Sir Almwroth, *143*
Zola, Emile, *195*

Image Copyright

Every effort has been made to identify relevant copyright holders of the images in this book, to obtain permission to reproduce them and to ensure that all credits are correct. We have acted in good faith and on the best information available to us at the time of publication. Any omissions are inadvertent, and will be corrected if notification is given in writing.

Printed in Great Britain by
Amazon.co.uk, Ltd.,
Marston Gate.